JOSEPH PRINCE

100 DAYS

—— of ——

RIGHT BELIEVING

Daily readings from *The Power of Right Believing*

*A guide to help you live free
from fear, guilt, and addiction*

*Faith
Words*

New York | Boston | Nashville

FaithWords
Hachette Book Group
237 Park Avenue
New York, NY 10017

www.faithwords.com

Printed in the United States of America

First Edition: February 2014
10 9 8 7 6 5 4 3 2 1

FaithWords is a division of Hachette Book Group, Inc.
The FaithWords name and logo are trademarks of Hachette Book Group, Inc.

The Hachette Speakers Bureau provides a wide range of authors for speaking events. To find out more, go to www.hachettespeakersbureau.com or call (866) 376-6591.

The publisher is not responsible for websites (or their content) that are not owned by the publisher.

Library of Congress Cataloging-in-Publication Data

ISBN: 978-1-4555-5713-4
LCCN: 2013954161

Introduction

My friend, I've got an invitation and a challenge for you that I believe will change your life! Over the next 100 days, I'd like for you to take the journey of a lifetime together with me and explore the amazing width and length and depth and height of our Father's unconditional love for us. God wants us to live with joy overflowing, peace that surpasses understanding, and an unshakable confidence in what He has done for us, but the noise, chaos, clutter, and busyness of life so often overwhelm and obscure the truth. Too often we live life not conscious of His love, and end up trapped in a vicious cycle of wrong believing that results in defeat, guilt, fears, and addictions.

All I ask is that over the next 100 days you simply set aside 15 minutes a day and discover what God really sees when He looks at you as His beloved child. I know from personal experience and the many amazing testimonies from people across America and around the world that your life will never be the same again. Start your day with God by saying, "Father, I thank You that this is going to be a great day with You!" Then make yourself a nice warm mug of coffee and invite Jesus to an intimate chat as you pick up this book. I believe that within these precious moments your life can be transformed and renewed as you allow God's Word to refresh and reshape your thinking, speaking, and decision making, and put unwavering hope in your heart. And when your mind is set to believe in God's love for you, you will let go of the life of defeat and step into a life full of victory, security, and success.

My friend, the transformation and breakthroughs you want to see in your life all begin with *what you believe*. Right believing holds the secret to changing your life: *If you can change what you believe, you can change your life!* Can this really be true? Can it really be so simple? Yes, my friend, because right believing is really all about looking to the person of Jesus. When you *believe* in Him—in His love for you, His grace toward you, and the power of His finished work in your life—*He* will transform you from the inside out. And we know that real change and breakthroughs can only come from the inside out.

Today, I invite you to journey with me to discover the powerful truths of God's Word that will unlock doors and lead you into the fullness of life that is found in Jesus and His love. Your life will be touched and transformed when you encounter His presence and allow your mind to be renewed with right beliefs about your true identity in Him. You'll find inspiration, hope, and encouragement to break free from all that is holding you back from the abundant life that God has planned for you. I am confident that you'll find the freedom and power you need to live your life to the fullest!

100 Days of Right Believing is based on my book, *The Power of Right Believing.* Each bite-sized inspirational reading includes:

• ***Today's Scripture***—A scripture that relates to the inspirational reading, giving it a biblical foundation and helping you to understand the truths presented. I encourage you to meditate on each scripture for the day. You'll be surprised how much the Holy Spirit will open up God's Word to you and refresh your heart!

• ***Today's Inspirational Excerpt*** from *The Power of Right Believing*— A key truth or nugget that will renew your mind and help you develop positive habits for right believing. These truths cover what it means to believe in God's love for you and receive His complete forgiveness. They also teach you how to win the battle for your mind and find rest in the Father's love.

• ***Today's Prayer***—Don't know what or how to pray for a breakthrough? These prayers will help you express all that's in your heart to your heavenly Father. Feel free to adapt them to your own situation. Just speak from your heart. The effective, fervent prayer of a child of God avails much. Your Father is waiting and listening!

• ***Today's Reflection on Right Believing***—As you prayerfully read each day's inspirational word, take time to journal the things that the Holy Spirit brings to your attention. Meditate on these things, as well as the person of Jesus and His love and grace toward you.

No matter where you are at or what challenges you face, for the next 100 days, I'm asking you to allow the Scriptures to speak to your heart. Be still and listen to what God is saying to you…let His words of grace saturate your spirit, soul, and mind. Day by day, the shackles of wrong believing will begin to loosen and fall off your life. Your thoughts and beliefs will begin to line up with the Lord's precious thoughts and promises toward you, and your bondages will fall off like dead leaves—all through the power of right believing!

My friend, I can't wait for you to get started on your journey of right believing! When you start to believe right in God's grace and goodness toward you, fears, guilt, and addictions will lose their hold on your life as His love, peace, and life begin to fill and flow through you.

So what are you waiting for? Let's get started!

Grace always,

Joseph Prince

DAY 1

What You Believe Matters

Today's Scripture

*"A good man out of the good treasure of his heart
brings forth good things, and an evil man out of the
evil treasure brings forth evil things."*
MATTHEW 12:35

Over the last two decades, I've had the privilege of ministering to precious people from all walks of life. I've had the honor of meeting people in my congregation and at conferences around the world and hearing their stories. For those whom I didn't get to meet in person, their letters and emails to me told their stories.

Stories of liberation from years of anxiety and depression. Stories of being rescued from the prison of fear. Stories of breaking loose from destructive habits and addictions.

Yet, for every person who found their breakthrough, I also know of many who are still struggling today. They are bound by severe insecurities, trapped by all kinds of disorders, and gripped by constant fear. They've tried every solution they can think of, but are still desperately clawing to be freed from their emotional and physical prisons.

How did those who experienced victory break free? Why are others still trapped?

The answer is simple but powerful: their *beliefs*. What you believe is critical.

You see, if you believe wrong, you will struggle with wrong thoughts. Wrong thoughts will produce unhealthy emotions that will lead to toxic feelings of guilt, shame, condemnation, and fear. And those wrong feelings will ultimately produce wrong behaviors, actions, and painful addictions.

Wrong believing starts you on a path of defeat. It is what keeps you trapped and drives you deeper and deeper into paralyzing captivity. Right believing, on the other hand, is the door out of this vicious cycle of defeat. When you believe right, you will live right. Right believing always produces right living.

Today, begin to believe right by choosing to know and believe in the powerful truths of God's Word and in His love for you. In the days to come, set your heart to discover and meditate on the Savior you have in Christ and what He has already accomplished for you. Choose to renew your mind with God's truths about who you really are in Christ and how precious you are to Him. I pray that as you begin to encounter the person of Jesus, you *will* begin to experience your breakthrough and lasting victory!

Today's Thought

What I believe matters. When I believe right, I will live right.

Today's Prayer

Father, because what I believe is so important, help me to renew my mind with right beliefs based on eternal truths from Your holy Word. I believe that my heart and mind are important to You. Open my eyes to see Your grace and Your love for me. Fill my mind with the good thoughts You have toward me today. I trust the Holy Spirit to lead me to right living and victory as I anchor my thoughts and beliefs on Your grace and Your Word. Amen.

Today's Reflection on Right Believing

DAY 2

Getting Control

Today's Scripture
"…and as you have believed, so let it be done for you."
MATTHEW 8:13

Whether you are aware of it or not, what you believe affects how you live your life. What you believe determines how you think, how you perceive a situation, and, ultimately, what course of action you take.

I've said this time and time again, and time and time again, I've also seen this principle borne out in people's lives: Right believing always produces right living. This means that if you want to see right living in your life, you need to understand the importance of believing right. When you believe right, you can't help but live right.

You see, people are struggling to control their behaviors and actions because they don't have control over their emotions and feelings. They don't have control over their emotions and feelings because they don't have control over their thoughts. And they don't have control over their thoughts because they are not controlling what they believe.

The converse is true. When you begin to believe right about God and in His love for you, you begin to change the way you see yourself and your situation. You'll stop feeling hopeless. You'll begin to lose your fears. And you'll respond differently to negative people and situations.

This is why God wants you anchored in the powerful truths of His Word to believe in His love for you. Your heavenly Father wants you to believe that He is for you and not against you. He wants you to know and believe that He is on your side, rooting for your success and propelling you toward your breakthrough with His love and tender mercies. He wants you to open your eyes to see what He sees when He looks at you—His beloved child.

My friend, I encourage you to take time to meditate on the truths in each of these daily readings. I believe that as you do, you'll see old defeatist thinking habits falling away. You'll find the most stubborn of addictions supernaturally annihilated. And you'll find a confident expectation of good for your future and destiny in Christ strengthening your heart and creating amazing days ahead for you!

Today's Thought

Right believing produces right living. When I begin to believe right, my thoughts, actions, and behavior will start to become right and bear good fruit in my life.

Today's Prayer

Father, thank You for the truth of Your Word that shows me and liberates me into every blessing Your Son, Jesus, has already purchased for me. As I choose to meditate on Your love and grace toward me, let Your Word bring healing to my soul and hope to my heart. Let me see by Your Spirit how much You love me, how You are always for me and how You desire to protect, deliver, and bless me. I believe and declare that my days ahead will be days filled with good because You love me. Amen.

Today's Reflection on Right Believing

DAY 3

Prison Break

Today's Scripture

Then they cried out to the LORD *in their trouble, and He saved them out of their distresses. He brought them out of darkness and the shadow of death, and broke their chains in pieces.*
PSALM 107:13–14

Who do you think you are? Have you forgotten all the mistakes you've made? Things will never get better. You should just accept your lot.

It's not going to work—you are just going to fail again!

Nobody loves you. You are all alone.

Have you been at the receiving end of these words of discouragement, accusation, and dismissal?

I've seen these tactics of deception, loaded with condemning judgment, used too many times by the adversary. I've seen too many people, who have tried to move out from under the shadow of their past or break free from their addictions, end up succumbing to these lies about themselves, their identity, and their future and their destiny. As a result, they are unable to break free, and day after day, they simply live to perpetuate the pain, fears, and addictions to which they're bound.

That's the power of *wrong* believing.

Wrong believing puts people in a prison—a prison where its inmates behave as though they are incarcerated in a maximum-security penitentiary. They march inexorably to their dank cells of self-doubt and addictions. They allow themselves to be led into dungeons of destructive behaviors. They have convinced themselves never to dream of a better place, believing that they have no choice but to live in despair, frustration, and defeat.

If that describes you, it's time for a prison break, my friend. It's time to break free from the crippling grip of all that has held you back. How? Through right believing—the light that illuminates the path of freedom out of this prison.

Know and believe that God does not want you to live imprisoned by fears, guilt, and addictions. Open your heart to believe His plan for you is to live with joy overflowing, peace that surpasses understanding, and an unshakable confidence in what He has done for you. Through the cross, Jesus has paid for you to have His abundant life—a life marked by His liberty, His power, and His blessings.

It's time to let go of the life of defeat and step into a life full of victory, security, and God's abundant grace!

Today's Thought
*God does not want me to live imprisoned by fears,
guilt, and addictions, but with joy, peace, and confidence
in what He has done for me.*

Today's Prayer
*Father, I thank You that You are breaking the chains of all
wrong believing that have kept me bound and freeing me more
and more to live an abundant life. I declare that as I learn more
of Your grace and good plans for my life, You are transforming me
from the inside out. I believe that as You begin to replace my
wrong beliefs with right beliefs from Your Word, my life
cannot but change for the better! Amen.*

Today's Reflection on Right Believing

DAY 4

Under the Care of the Good Shepherd

Today's Scripture

*The LORD is my shepherd; I shall not want. He makes me to
lie down in green pastures; He leads me beside the still waters.
He restores my soul; He leads me in the paths of righteousness for
His name's sake. Yea, though I walk through the valley of the
shadow of death, I will fear no evil; for You are with me;
Your rod and Your staff, they comfort me.*
PSALM 23:1–4

If we're honest, we all have some measure of wrong believing in our lives. Just ask yourself, "Have I often felt anxious, worried, or fearful that the worst would happen to me and my loved ones?" These negative, exhausting emotions are merely flags that indicate what we truly believe about ourselves, our lives, and God.

When we are fearful and worried all the time, we are living as if we don't believe that we have a strong and able Shepherd who is tenderhearted toward us, who leads us to good places, who protects us and lovingly watches over us. So if worrying or being fearful seems to be your natural default mode, what you need to do is to keep hearing and learning about how much God loves you, and how precious you are to Him.

That is why the way out of constant worrying is not a matter of just thinking positively; it's birthed out of knowing you have a personal and intimate relationship with a loving Savior who watches over your needs and tends to you as a loving Shepherd. The more strongly you believe that He is taking care of you, the more it will change your thoughts and feelings, and the less you will fall victim to unhealthy emotions and behaviors.

Today, if you need freedom from a bad situation, see Jesus, your good Shepherd, leading you out of it by His Word that brings life and illumination. The psalmist says it this way: "Your word is a lamp to my feet and a light to my path" (Ps. 119:105). In The Message translation, it says, "By your words I can see where I'm going; they throw a beam of light on my dark path."

My friend, the Lord wants to throw a beam of light on your path today. Whatever you are struggling with presently, no matter how insurmountable your challenges appear, when you start believing right, things are going to start turning around for your good!

Today's Thought

I can live life confident and at peace because Jesus, my strong and able Shepherd, is watching over me.

Today's Prayer

Lord Jesus, thank You for being my good Shepherd and watching over me. Thank You for defending and protecting me when I'm helpless, and providing for me when I'm in lack. Thank You for leading me with Your Word and wisdom whenever I'm in doubt and don't know what to do. With You as my Shepherd, I don't have to live life worried about my needs or my future. I believe You will cause me to walk in green pastures of provision and rest and to always see Your goodness. Amen.

Today's Reflection on Right Believing

DAY 5

The Truth That Frees You

Today's Scripture

"And you shall know the truth, and the truth shall make you free."
JOHN 8:32

The very premise of this book is based on the truth of John 8:32, but what does "the truth shall make you free" really mean?

Examine the context of this verse and you'll notice that Jesus said this to the Jews of His day. These were people who at an early age grew up studying and learning the law. Yet, these people, in ways very similar to us today, still battled with fears, anxieties, sicknesses, and all kinds of oppression, bondages, and addictions. So this truth that Jesus was talking about clearly cannot be the law, because these people could not find freedom in the law. In fact, the truth of the law only brought them into religious bondage.

My friend, the truth that *shall make you free*, is the truth of His grace. This is the truth that He came to give us. His Word proclaims that "grace and truth came through Jesus Christ" (John 1:17).

The good news is that grace came to set you free from the curse of the law. Grace is not a doctrine or a theological subject. When Jesus talks about grace, He is talking about Himself. Grace is a person. Grace is Jesus Himself.

The truth that has the power to fling wide open your prison doors is His grace. His grace is the antidote to counteract every poison in your mind! When you encounter Jesus, taste His love, and savor His loving-kindness and tender mercies, every wrong belief begins to dissolve in the glory of His love. And every dark thought and evil addiction that may have held you captive cannot but scatter when it is exposed to the light of His grace!

Your freedom is found in rightly believing in Jesus—His favor and His love in your life. When you believe right about His grace, you will begin to live right. The more you see in His Word what His grace has done for you, the more fears, condemnation, depression, and destructive habits will lose their grip in your life. And the more you believe and enjoy His grace and love, the

19

more you'll find the Lord's wisdom, stability, and peace guiding your decisions and actions.

Right believing always produces right living and the right results.

Today's Thought
The truth that sets me free is not the truth of the law,
but the truth of grace—the person of Jesus.

Today's Prayer
Father, thank You for the truth of Your grace that counteracts every
poison in my mind. I receive and rest in Your love and grace for me
today. I believe that it's not the law, but Your abundant grace, that
sets me free from all fears, condemning thoughts, and addictions.
Let me see more and more of Jesus. Let me receive more and more
of His love, His grace, and His goodness so that I may truly
walk in His liberty in every area of my life. Amen.

Today's Reflection on Right Believing

DAY 6

Grace Can Uproot That Addiction for Good

Today's Scripture

*"…the L*ORD* has anointed Me to preach good tidings to the poor;*
He has sent Me to heal the brokenhearted, to proclaim liberty to the
captives, and the opening of the prison to those who are bound."

ISAIAH 61:1

Kate was addicted to alcohol as well as dependent on a cocktail of strong antidepressants, tranquilizers, beta-blockers, and sleeping pills. Over time, trying to cope with the high-octane demands of being a corporate highflier as well as the strain of maintaining her success and image had driven her to look for relief from all these sources. To the rest of the world, Kate appeared to have it all together. But in reality, her despair over her inability to cope without those substances only plunged her into a vicious cycle of defeat.

Kate tried everything to beat the bottle and her depression: She made appointments with psychiatrists and psychologists and even faithfully attended support groups for alcoholics. Through these endless appointments and meetings, she experienced what she calls "a few bouts of recovery" that lasted several days at best.

In the end, Kate found herself on the verge of giving up. But God had other plans for her. He led her to one of the leaders in my church who encouraged her to keep hearing the preached Word and praying in the Spirit. And as she kept listening to my messages on God's grace, God began uprooting the wrong beliefs that had taken hold in Kate's mind and replacing them with right beliefs about herself and her future.

The more she heard, the more she was able to keep her eyes on Jesus, instead of trying to overcome the symptoms. The more she heard, the more she was able to be at rest, to see God's blessings in the little things, and to supernaturally not even experience withdrawal symptoms. And in a short time, four long and treacherous years of addiction to alcohol disappeared for Kate.

The same can happen for you. In a supernatural instant, you too can experience liberation from destructive habits, fears, and bondages. You may not be able to understand how grace can set you free from a long-term addiction, but you *can* experience it in your heart and experience His liberty in your area of challenge!

Today's Thought

The more I hear and believe God's grace for me, the more wrong beliefs are uprooted in my life, and the more I shall experience victory supernaturally.

Today's Prayer

Father, I thank You that Your grace has only good in store for me. I know that You love me and that You have wonderful plans for me. In the midst of my challenge, I receive Your grace, Your liberty, and Your deliverance. Help me to keep my eyes on You and the truth of Your grace instead of my circumstances. I believe that by Your grace alone, I will walk triumphantly above every negative circumstance and experience the freedom and blessings Christ has purchased for me. Amen.

Today's Reflection on Right Believing

DAY 7

A Jesus-Encounter Can Free You Supernaturally

Today's Scripture

*And behold, there was a woman who had a spirit of
infirmity eighteen years, and was bent over and could in no
way raise herself up. But when Jesus saw her, He called her to Him
and said to her, "Woman, you are loosed from your infirmity."
And He laid His hands on her, and immediately she was
made straight, and glorified God.*
Luke 13:11–13

After reading Kate's story yesterday, you may be asking, "How can this be? How does four years of alcohol addiction just disappear like that? How could such a powerful craving just lose its hold in such a short time?"

The answer is simple but powerful.

Kate allowed God's love to invade her mind as she listened to grace-based messages on her iPod that were full of Jesus and His love. My friend, when you allow His love to saturate your mind, it doesn't matter what wrong beliefs, fears, or addictions are keeping you bound. God's grace will begin to break them down. This is what happens when you have an encounter with your loving Savior. Everyone who encounters Jesus never leaves the same. He came to set the captives free.

Whatever your condition, however long it has kept you bound—two years, ten years, thirty years—I want you to know and believe that God can set you free in a supernatural instant. Believe that the One who is both willing and able to set you free is the same one who created time, and He who created time isn't time-bound. He who turned water into the finest aged wine in a matter of seconds can bypass natural processes and accelerate your deliverance from any bondage!

I know of many people who struggled with addictions for decades. But once they had a supernatural encounter with Jesus, they just woke up one morning and found themselves free, with none of that familiar urge or desire to engage in their negative behavior anymore. Frank, who lives in the state of Maryland, wrote to me and shared how he was set free from drug addiction. He had been told "once an addict, always an addict," and he had believed it.

But when he came to know the truth about the life-transforming love and grace of Jesus through one of my teaching resources, it just destroyed the chains that bound him. He shared, "Man, I could have jumped through the roof when I discovered that all I had to do was accept the finished work of Jesus and His grace! After thirty years of drug addiction, I thought there was no hope for me. But praise Jesus, I am now drug-free, and I'm in a good grace-preaching church with my wife, who has also been set free of her drug addiction."

My friend, that is the power of right believing!

Today, believe God loves you and that His grace is available for you. Whatever bad prognosis you may have heard about your situation, no matter how dark and dire your circumstances may be right now, believe and accept God's grace. You don't have to accept defeat for the rest of your life!

Today's Thought
Jesus came to set me free from every bondage. He is my deliverer and my liberty today.

Today's Prayer
Father, fill my heart and mind with Your perfect love and peace as I continue to read and listen to Your words of life. Give me a fresh encounter with Your Son, Jesus. Open my heart to see and know His perfect love and immeasurable grace for me. As I choose to see how He is my liberty, my answer, and my deliverer, I believe You are supernaturally driving out every fear, wrong belief, and addiction in my life. Amen.

Today's Reflection on Right Believing

DAY 8

Presenting the Real God

Today's Scripture

When He had come down from the mountain, great multitudes
followed Him. And behold, a leper came and worshiped Him,
saying, "Lord, if You are willing, You can make me clean." Then
Jesus put out His hand and touched him, saying, "I am willing;
be cleansed." Immediately his leprosy was cleansed.
MATTHEW 8:1–3

There is so much wrong believing today about who Jesus is. I am asking you to throw out every idea, concept, and picture that you may have of a "religious" Jesus. Allow me to introduce the real Jesus to you, for this is where it all begins. I'm not talking about the religious Jesus you may have heard about growing up, but the real Jesus who walked along the dusty streets of Jerusalem and upon the raging waters of the Galilee.

He was the one whom the sick, the poor, the sinful, the down and out, and the outcast instinctively gravitated to and felt at ease with. He was God in the flesh and He manifested God's tangible love. In His presence, those who were imperfect didn't feel fearful of Him, or sense judgment or condemnation from Him. To those who sought Him for healing, restoration, and supply—no matter what their past or background—He always extended a loving, compassionate heart and hand to them and oversupplied their need.

Contrary to what a lot of people think, you don't have to be "religious" to have access to God and His help. In fact, the less "religious" you are, the better. The real Jesus didn't come to bring a new religion. He didn't come to be served and waited upon. No, He came to serve, and serve He did.

The real Jesus created the universe with one command and orchestrated the paths of each planet so that none would collide. He had every right to demand service from those He created, yet He supplied service. He bowed down and with His own hands washed the grime and filth from His disciples' feet. Those same hands would later be pierced with coarse nails at the cross, and He would with His own blood wash us of the grime and filth of all our sins by taking them upon His own body. What a far cry from the condemning, judgmental, faultfinding God whom many have portrayed Him to be!

This is the true Jesus—totally unlike what many of us have been taught about God. He is willing and able to meet your need today and love you into wholeness.

Today's Thought
With all of my imperfections and needs, I can come unafraid into the presence of the real Jesus, and discover His love for me.

Today's Prayer
Father, open my eyes to see and know more of Your beloved Son— not a "religious" Jesus who is distant, legalistic, and condemning, but the real Jesus who is altogether lovely, full of grace, mercy, and truth toward me and my family. Keep showing me His beauty, love, and grace and draw me into a more intimate and loving relationship with Him every day. Thank You, Father. Amen.

Today's Reflection on Right Believing

DAY 9

Believe in a God of Grace

Today's Scripture

Let us therefore come boldly to the throne of grace, that we may obtain mercy and find grace to help in time of need.
HEBREWS 4:16

Are you like many today who believe in a "religious" God? Do you believe that God is against you when you fall short, that He is angry with you when you fail, and that fellowship with Him is cut off when you make mistakes?

It's no wonder then that instead of running to the one true solution, many sincere folks run in the opposite direction when they are hurting. So there is a great deception, a powerful, wrong belief about God that has trapped many in the vicious cycle of condemnation, guilt, fear, defeat, and addiction.

My friend, I want you to know today that God is a God of infinite grace. He is repugnant to the "religious," but gracious and irresistible to those who are hurting.

No matter what you are going through today, whatever addictions may be binding you, right believing can and will set you free. Start with believing this powerful truth:

God is a God of grace and forgiveness. He loves you very much, and He doesn't hold your mistakes against you.

Don't let the mistakes you have made in the past hold you back from reaching out to God and receiving His forgiveness for all your failures. Begin to believe right about the Lord, believe right about His heart and love for you, and your entire life will be transformed. Right believing always leads to right living!

Today's Thought

God is a God of grace and forgiveness. He loves me very much and doesn't hold my mistakes against me.

Today's Prayer

Father, I thank You that You are a God of infinite grace. And because of Jesus' sacrifice for me, I can run to You boldly to obtain mercy and find help whenever I have failed or am feeling discouraged. Fellowship with You is never broken. Thank You for Your complete forgiveness. Thank You for not ever holding my mistakes against me, for caring when I am hurting, and for always being my supply in every situation of need and lack. Amen.

Today's Reflection on Right Believing

DAY 10

Pursued by God

Today's Scripture

*But He needed to go through Samaria. So He came to a city of
Samaria which is called Sychar...Now Jacob's well was there. Jesus
therefore, being wearied from His journey, sat thus by the well.
It was about the sixth hour. A woman of Samaria came to
draw water. Jesus said to her, "Give Me a drink."*
JOHN 4:4–7

I encourage you to read the remarkable story of the Samaritan woman in John 4. Considered a woman with a shady past, she was gossiped about in her village and probably shunned for being a home wrecker, a "stealer of husbands." Now, hers is not a fictional story. She was a real person, just like you and me. Her problems and pain, like many of ours, were real and hounded her every day...until she encountered a very real Savior!

Despite the custom of the Jews of that day to avoid any contact with the Samaritans, whom they perceived as spiritually inferior, John records that as Jesus was traveling from Judea to Galilee, "He *had* to go through Samaria" (John 4:4 NLT, emphasis mine). Pause with me and think about these words for a moment: *Had to. Needed to. Must.* Words that speak not just of necessity, but underscore a steady resolve and even urgency! Jesus had deliberately scheduled a divine appointment with the woman at the well, though she knew nothing about it.

We know from the account that this ostracized, lonely woman had a life-transforming conversation with Jesus at the well. But make no mistake—it wasn't she who sought out Jesus to talk to Him. It was the Savior who pursued the one whom others shunned. Do you know that He is still doing that today?

Do you have a past that you are ashamed of? Are you struggling to overcome something that you know is destroying you? Do you feel all alone and that no one understands the pain you are going through?

I want you to know that Jesus hasn't changed. As He was for the Samaritan woman, the loving Savior is still your very present help in your time of need (see Ps. 46:1). He knows the suffering, shame, and struggles you are going through right now. And even if what you are going through is a consequence of bad life choices and mistakes of your own doing, He doesn't abandon and forsake you. No—a thousand times, no! He goes out of the way to have a personal appointment with you, to restore and rescue you. The fact that you are reading this right now is a confirmation that Jesus is reaching out to you with His love, grace, and forgiveness.

Talk to Him as the woman did. Taste and touch His grace and compassion for you as she did. And like her, discover Jesus' forgiveness, freedom, and strength to walk into a bright new future.

Today's Thought

*Right now, Jesus is reaching out to me with His love,
grace, and forgiveness.*

Today's Prayer

*Lord Jesus, I thank You that although You know every detail
about my life—all my past mistakes and all my present struggles—
You still love me so much that You pursue me. I praise You for
seeking me even when I had no idea that You cared. I believe You are
reaching out to me right now, and I receive Your love, Your grace,
and Your forgiveness. I look to You, Jesus, to be my wisdom,
peace, and strength every day. Amen.*

Today's Reflection on Right Believing

DAY 11

When the Storms of Life Rage

Today's Scripture

God is our refuge and strength, a very present help in trouble.
PSALM 46:1

Storms of life. You know them well. They overwhelm you. Wave after wave of relentless battering that knocks you off your feet till you don't know which side is up. Till every ounce of energy is used up and you feel so weak, abandoned, and lonely. Perhaps you're caught in one of life's storms right now.

When the disciples of Jesus were out at sea, caught in a turbulent tempest and tossed by the waves, who came to them in their darkest hour? It was Jesus Himself (see Matt. 14:22–33). Jesus came in style, walking on the raging waters. The loving Savior came to them at their exact point of need to rescue them.

What does this tell you? That He is above the storms. He walks above— He is greater than—every adversity and opposition that you may be facing right now, and He comes to you to rescue you!

With the billowing waves beneath His feet, His first words to His disciples were, "Don't be afraid. Take courage. I am here!" (Matt. 14:27 NLT). What comfort those words must have brought to the disciples who were exhausted and shaking with fear for their lives.

My friend, when the storms of life rage, don't go by what you see and hear all around you. Don't go by your negative feelings and emotions. Live by the truth of God's Word, which encourages you to "be strong and courageous! Do not be afraid and do not panic…For the LORD your God will personally go ahead of you. He will neither fail you nor abandon you" (Deut. 31:6 NLT). Our God is a personal and loving God who is with you in your boat right in the midst of the howling storm. He knows how to lead you to victory every time. He cannot fail you!

Today's Thought

God, who cannot fail me, is with me in my boat. He knows what storms are ahead and will lead me to victory every time!

Today's Prayer

Lord Jesus, I acknowledge that when the storms of life rock my boat, it's so easy to get into fear and panic. Thank You for reminding me today that You are watching over me, that You are here to rescue me, and that the winds and the waves are no problem for You. I believe Your Word is true, and I believe You are calling me to take courage in Your presence. Open my eyes, Lord, and help me to see that You are always with me, and how You are above every storm. I welcome You into my boat, and I declare that no matter how bad the storm may seem right now, I am not going down, because You cannot fail me! Amen.

Today's Reflection on Right Believing

DAY 12

A Door of Hope

Today's Scripture

"I will return her vineyards to her and transform the
Valley of Trouble into a gateway of hope…"
HOSEA 2:15 NLT

Are you among the people who think that when you fail, God leaves you and only returns when you get your act together? Some people think that they must clean up their lives and overcome all their struggles on their own before they can come before the presence of God. Well, I have a simple question for you: Do you clean yourself before you take a bath? Of course not!

In the same way, God wants you to come to Him just as you are, with all your weaknesses, idiosyncrasies, wrong beliefs, hang-ups, and all your bondages, fears, and addictions. He is the bath! You don't have to try to clean yourself up before you come to Him.

But Pastor Prince, what if the mess I'm in is entirely of my own doing? Can I still just come to God as I am and expect Him to help me?

Yes, even if your trouble is due to your own willfulness or a mistake of your own making, He is still with you. He has never left you, and He never will. He will never forsake you (see Heb. 13:5). You are precious in His eyes. Can you imagine living life with the kind of confidence, assurance, and peace that comes when you are truly anchored in this truth?

Today, even if you find yourself in the Valley of Trouble, know that you will not remain there for long. You will walk through it and not remain or camp there (see Ps. 23:4). God is opening a door of hope in your life today for you to step out of your darkness and into His marvelous light (see 1 Pet. 2:9). Things are going to get better. The breakthroughs that you have been waiting for are coming your way. Step through the door of hope and out of your Valley of Trouble today. Jesus is your door of hope! Believe in His love for you and allow Him to lead you to freedom. In His loving presence, you will find forgiveness, healing, and restoration. He will mend your life and transform you from the inside out.

Today's Thought

I am precious in God's eyes. He who knows me perfectly loves me perfectly! I can come to Jesus just as I am and receive His help.

Today's Prayer

Father, I can't clean myself up from the messes I've made in my life, and I can't find my way out of the Valley of Trouble on my own. I've tried and failed over and over again. Thank You for Your promise that You will transform my troubles into a door of hope because of Jesus. I believe that You are extending Your hand of grace and love to me and that You will mend my life and transform me from the inside out. I take Your hand and step out of my darkness into Your marvelous light. Amen.

Today's Reflection on Right Believing

DAY 13

Go to the Source

Today's Scripture

The LORD is merciful and gracious, slow to anger, and abounding in mercy…. He has not dealt with us according to our sins, nor punished us according to our iniquities. For as the heavens are high above the earth, so great is His mercy toward those who fear Him; as far as the east is from the west, so far has He removed our transgressions from us.

PSALM 103:8, 10–12

Psalm 103 is one of my favorite psalms of David, a beautiful psalm that describes who and what God really is—a gracious and merciful Savior. Believing right begins with what you believe about God and must be based on the solid foundation of God's Word. To know the truth about who and what God is, we can't go by feelings, circumstances, human conjectures, or what we may have heard someone say about God. We have to go to the source!

If you heard a rumor that someone you knew was saying horrible and negative things about you, don't believe it immediately. Go to the source first. Ask this person if this is what he or she really said or if this is what he or she really meant. Many people allow precious friendships and relationships to become fractured because they believe the rumors. They become bitter, angry, and disappointed without ever verifying with the person if he or she had actually said those nasty things.

In the same way, in the world we live in, there are all kinds of wrong beliefs perpetuated about God: "God is angry at you." "He is disappointed with you." "God is allowing all these negative things to happen to you because He's punishing you for your past sins."

Please do NOT believe all this baseless gossip about God! Such impressions of God have damaged many people's relationships with Him, and they live with a distorted perspective of who God really is. Instead of receiving His love, grace, and forgiveness, they become afraid, distant, and fearful of Him. Instead of allowing Jesus to come into their situations, they live their lives running away, avoiding, and hiding from Him.

Come on, let's honor God and go to the source. Look again at what the Bible says about Him in today's Scripture reading: He is "slow to anger, and abounding in mercy…as far as the east is from the west, so far has He removed our transgressions from us." *This* is our God! *This* is why you can always run to Him and believe that you can freely receive His help!

Today's Thought
According to God's Word, God is slow to anger
and abounding in mercy toward me.

Today's Prayer
Father, thank You for Your Word that is truth. I acknowledge
that in the past I have bought into many of the world's wrong beliefs,
distortions, and lies about You, and that I've run away from You
rather than to You. Today, I choose to believe that You are gracious
and merciful, slow to anger, and abounding in mercy toward me.
I believe that as far as the east is from the west, so far have You
removed my sins from me. Help me to always see You as the
God of love and compassion that You really are, and come
boldly to receive Your mercy and grace. Amen.

Today's Reflection on Right Believing

DAY 14

If You Only Knew

Today's Scripture

"If you only knew the gift God has for you and who you are speaking to, you would ask me, and I would give you living water…. Anyone who drinks this water [from the well] will soon become thirsty again. But those who drink the water I give will never be thirsty again. It becomes a fresh, bubbling spring within them, giving them eternal life."
JOHN 4:10, 13–14 NLT

Remember the shunned Samaritan woman whose story you read on Day 10? When she asked Jesus why He (a Jew) would ask her (a despised Samaritan) for a drink of water, this was His amazing response: that she would ask *Him* for living water, the only thing that would satisfy her from within and slake her deep thirst for acceptance and love forever.

What an amazing Savior! Although this woman had a past of looking for love in all the wrong places that imprisoned her in shame and self-loathing, Jesus met her at her point of greatest need with the offer of Himself, the living water. He knew all that she had ever done and yet offered her the true intimacy that fully satisfies every aching need. He invited her to discover, taste, and experience His perfect and unconditional love.

Jesus is saying the same thing to you today: *If you only knew* who it is who comes to you in your darkest and weakest moments. *If you only knew* this gift of God who will never leave you nor forsake you, who has gone before you and who comes to you in the midst of your storms. *If you only knew* the One who reaches out to you even when you have failed and who doesn't hold your past mistakes or present failures against you.

Beloved, if you only knew this gift of God who offers the living water of His unconditional, endless love to you and you drink of that love, you will never thirst again. You won't need to look for love or acceptance in all the wrong places, have your heart broken and fearful about the future, and have your life derailed. You can wake up with a fresh expectation of good every day.

43

Jesus was essentially inviting the woman to ask Him for the living water of His love. Will you do that today? Your life will never be the same again when you personally experience His love!

Today's Thought
Jesus offers me the living water of His unconditional, endless love today. My life will never be the same again when I personally experience His love!

Today's Prayer
Lord Jesus, I am so thirsty for You. I know that only You can satisfy the deepest needs of my heart. Today, I believe that You are here right now, offering me the living water of Your love. I receive Your love and Your life into my heart and into my life. Thank You for reaching out to me, and for Your perfect and unconditional love that will never fail me. I receive You as the answer to all I will ever need for every challenge that I face. Amen.

Today's Reflection on Right Believing

DAY 15

"Jesus Loves Me! This I Know…"

Today's Scripture

The LORD has appeared of old to me, saying:
"Yes, I have loved you with an everlasting love; therefore
with lovingkindness I have drawn you."

JEREMIAH 31:3

I heard a story of a minister from Oregon who was assigned to provide counseling in a state mental institution. His first assignment was to a padded cell that housed deranged, barely clothed patients. He couldn't even talk to the inmates, let alone counsel them—the only responses he got were groans, moans, and demonic laughter.

Then the Holy Spirit prompted him to sit in the middle of the room and for a full hour just sing the famous children's hymn that goes, "Jesus loves me! This I know, for the Bible tells me so. Little ones to Him belong; they are weak, but He is strong." Nothing happened at the end of that first day, but for weeks he persisted to sing the same melody with greater conviction each time: "Yes, Jesus loves me! Yes, Jesus loves me! Yes, Jesus loves me! The Bible tells me so."

As the days passed, the patients began singing with him one by one. Amazingly, by the end of the first month, thirty-six of the severely ill patients were transferred from the high-dependency ward to a self-care ward. Within a year, all but two were discharged from the mental institution.[1]

As one of the best-known and loved hymns of all time, this hymn's ongoing popularity lies in its succinct elegance in unveiling Jesus' heart. It beckons one to recognize that no matter what challenges, failures, and misdeeds one might be dealing with, *the love of Jesus remains a constant.*

"Jesus loves me! This I know."

How so?

"For the Bible tells me so."

So simple, yet so powerful.

Whether you feel it or not, Jesus' constant love for you rests in the truth and on the foundation of His unchanging Word. It proclaims that His love for you and me is based utterly and completely on Him—on His promises, His work, and His grace. Today, let healing and rest for your soul come as you allow your heart to be anchored on this truth.

Today's Thought

No matter what challenges, failures, and misdeeds I am dealing with, Jesus loves me! Yes, Jesus loves me! The Bible tells me so.

Today's Prayer

Lord Jesus, thank You for unveiling Your great heart of love for me in Your Word. I am amazed by how much You love me no matter what I have or have not done. I believe that Your love is true and constant and that nothing can change that. Today, I rest in Your love because it is based on the sure foundation of Your unchanging Word. Because You love me, You went to the cross for me. Because You love me, You are with me and for me today, supplying all that I need. Thank You, Jesus! Amen.

Today's Reflection on Right Believing

DAY 16

Who You Are in God's Eyes

Today's Scripture

We love Him because He first loved us.

1 JOHN 4:19

Do you believe that God loves you with an unchanging love today? Even if you've just failed or made a mistake? This, my friend, is where the rubber meets the road in our Christian walk every day.

I'm here to tell you beyond the shadow of a doubt that God loves you with an everlasting love. His love for you is unconditional (see Titus 3:3–5 NASB). It is a love that is so pure, pristine, and marvelous. It has nothing to do with your performance, but everything to do with who you are in His eyes—His beloved. The emphasis of the old covenant of the law was all about your love for God, whereas the emphasis of the new covenant of grace is all about God's love for you. The sum total of the law under the old covenant is, "You shall love the LORD your God with all your heart, with all your soul, and with all your strength" (Deut. 6:5, see also Matt. 22:37, 40).

Let's be honest here. Have you ever met anyone who can love God this way? Of course not. It's a human impossibility. The law was designed to show us that we are incapable of loving God perfectly.

Knowing that man wouldn't be able to fulfill His commandment to love Him with all his heart, all his soul, all his mind, and all his strength, do you know what God did? He demonstrated how only *He* could love us with all His heart, all His soul, all His mind, and all His strength when He sent His beloved Son, Jesus Christ, to redeem us from all our sins with His own blood. That is why the new covenant is all about God's love for you and not your love for Him! Under grace, God doesn't want you to focus your thoughts on, "Do I really love God?" That's not the focus of the new covenant. Under grace, God wants you to focus on *His* love for you. Therefore, the questions you should be asking yourself are:

"Do I know how much God loves me today?"
"Do I really believe that God loves me right now?"

49

Choose to believe right about how God loves you today. It makes all the difference in the world to how quickly you are able to get back on your feet, and go from faith to faith and strength to strength in your walk with Him.

Today's Thought

Under the new covenant of grace, God wants me to focus on His love for me.

Today's Prayer

Father, thank You that Your new covenant of grace is all about how much You love me unconditionally and not how able I am to love and please You. I praise You that You see me as Your beloved child and that You surround Me with Your unmerited favor. I believe that I am the apple of Your eye and the delight of Your heart. I rejoice that I am highly favored, greatly blessed, and deeply loved by You! Amen.

Today's Reflection on Right Believing

DAY 17

Nothing Means Nothing!

Today's Scripture

*For I am persuaded that neither death nor life, nor angels
nor principalities nor powers, nor things present nor things to come,
nor height nor depth, nor any other created thing, shall be able to
separate us from the love of God which is in Christ Jesus our Lord.*
ROMANS 8:38–39

I often hear people say, "God's love is unconditional!" But the moment they fail, all of a sudden, the love they once said was unconditional becomes contingent upon their behavior. Many believe that God loves them when they do right, but stops loving them the moment they do something wrong. Well, I'm going to shatter that wrong belief into smithereens with the truth of God's Word!

While our love for God can fluctuate, His love for us always remains constant. His love for us is based on who He is and not based on what we do. I love just how confident and emphatic the apostle Paul is when he says, "For I am persuaded that neither death nor life, nor angels nor principalities nor powers, nor things present nor things to come, nor height nor depth, nor any other created thing, shall be able to separate us from the love of God which is in Christ Jesus our Lord" (Rom. 8:38–39). In the New International Version, it says, "For I am convinced…"

Are you *persuaded* and *convinced* the way the apostle Paul is that as a child of God, nothing, not even your sins, failings, and mistakes, can ever separate you from the love of God? Don't go by what you feel, think, or have been taught. God's Word proclaims in no uncertain terms that nothing can separate you from His love. Nothing means *nothing*! His love for you is not contingent on your immaculate performance. He loves you even in your failings. That's why it is called grace! It is the undeserved, unmerited, and unearned favor of God. If you can deserve God's grace, then it is no longer grace.

So the next time you do something wrong, hold fast to His love as unconditional. Receive His love afresh, and you will have the power to overcome that failing—and every struggle—every time.

Today's Thought

*As a child of God, nothing, not even my sins, failings,
and mistakes, can ever separate me from His love.*

Today's Prayer

*Father, thank You for the assurance of Your Word that says
Your love for me is constant and that I never need to try to earn or be
worthy of Your grace. I praise You for Your grace—Your undeserved,
unmerited, and unearned favor in my life. I declare with the
apostle Paul that I am persuaded that nothing, absolutely nothing—
not my sins, failures, or mistakes—can ever separate me from
Your love in Christ Jesus, my Lord. I thank You I am completely
and irrevocably forgiven. Amen.*

Today's Reflection on Right Believing

DAY 18

It's All about God's Love

Today's Scripture

"Therefore I say to you, her sins, which are many, are forgiven, for she loved much. But to whom little is forgiven, the same loves little."

LUKE 7:47

Her story is heartrending. In the Bible's account, this woman is described as "a sinner" (Luke 7:37). Many believe that she was a prostitute. When she came to Jesus, He did not chase her away, humiliate her, or condemn her for her sins. He knew how guilt had been eating her up on the inside, and had compassion for her.

As she neared Jesus, she began weeping. Then, she washed His feet with her tears, wiped them with her hair, and anointed them with the precious ointment that would have cost her an entire year's wages. Without hesitation, she lavished it on Jesus' feet and worshiped Him.

In response, Jesus said that those who know and believe how abundantly God truly loves and has forgiven them will end up loving God very much. Simply put, those who have been forgiven much, love much. Those who have been forgiven little, love little. That's why the emphasis of the new covenant is not about your love for God; it is about God's love for you.

Do you see that your love for God in the new covenant is birthed out of a genuine and authentic relationship with Him? It is not a groveling display that is birthed out of the fear of punishment or religious obligation. Under grace, we are able to love God because He first loved us. That is why people under grace become the holiest people you will ever meet. Their holiness flows out of their love relationship with Jesus! They have experienced His unconditional love in an intimate and personal way that transforms them. They just want to live lives that glorify and honor the name of Jesus.

Friend, we have all been forgiven much, but many don't know and don't believe this. Give up on trying to overcome your own failings, mistakes, addictions, and bondages, imagining that God requires this of you before you can come before Him. When you fail, come to Jesus with boldness and confidence as this woman did. Feel free to weep in His sweet presence and simply worship Him. Pour out everything that is on your heart to Him. Don't worry, He will not heap more guilt and condemnation upon you. He will remind you of the cross and say, "Your sins are already forgiven. I have already paid the price for your sins at Calvary. Rest in My forgiveness and love for you."

Today's Thought
When I know and believe how abundantly God loves me and has forgiven me of all my sins, I will end up loving Him much!

Today's Prayer
Lord Jesus, thank You for paying the price for my sins at Calvary because You knew there's no way I could ever pay for them myself. Because of Your sacrifice at the cross, I don't have to be afraid to come to You when I've failed. And because You welcome me into Your presence, I come now before You with boldness. I lay all my sins, failings, addictions, and bondages at Your feet, and I receive Your forgiveness and power to overcome them. I believe that You love me and have already forgiven me. I worship and adore You, my precious Lord and Savior. Amen.

Today's Reflection on Right Believing

DAY 19

Destined to Reign

Today's Scripture

Oh, taste and see that the LORD is good; blessed is the man who trusts in Him!
PSALM 34:8

I received a letter from a man, whom I'll just call Patrick, who struggled with sexual addictions for more than ten years. He knew it was wrong, but he couldn't break free from those addictions no matter how hard he tried. His conscience would plague him with reminders of his sins every time he tried to read the Word. This fed his belief that he wasn't good enough for God and that God didn't want anything to do with him because of his addictions.

This man lived in this realm of self-torture day after day. Then one day he read one of my books, *Destined To Reign*. Through the book, he came to discover and believe in Jesus' finished work at the cross. He said, "I just decided to rest in Jesus' finished work, His forgiveness, His victory, His grace, and His love, *and pornography and masturbation now have no power or dominion over me*. It truly is awesome, especially because I had tried for more than ten years to get victory, and all it took was for me to know the truth and rest in Jesus' finished work. All glory to God!"

I don't know what guilt you may be struggling with today, but God does. You no longer have to live under the dictates of your conscience, which condemns you every time you miss the mark. See the blood of Jesus cleansing your heart, and be free from the prison of guilt to experience victory like this precious brother.

I encourage you to fill your heart with psalms, hymns, and spiritual songs that are full of God's love and grace. When your heart is full of Jesus, wrong beliefs will begin to be replaced by right beliefs. Destructive addictions will be replaced by new, positive habits. Fear, shame, and guilt will begin to dissolve in the warmth of His perfect love for you. Experience His love today!

Today's Thought

Victory comes when I know the truth of the Lord's grace
and rest in His finished work.

Today's Prayer

Father, You have destined me to have victory over every sin,
addiction, and fear in life through Jesus, Your Son. I come to You
and I choose to rest in the finished work of Jesus at the cross. I believe
His forgiveness, His victory, His grace, and His love are mine. I
receive Your perfect love and power to break free from all guilt,
condemnation, and shame. I am free in Jesus' name.
All praise and glory to You! Amen.

Today's Reflection on Right Believing

DAY 20

Play the Right Mental Movies

Today's Scripture

For I know the thoughts that I think toward you, says the Lord, *thoughts of peace and not of evil, to give you a future and a hope.*
JEREMIAH 29:11

I can still remember what happened when I visited a lady from my congregation in the hospital. Heather had suffered a stroke that completely paralyzed the left side of her body. As I prayed for her, she lifted her right hand in a gesture of prayer. Amazingly, her left hand followed suit, albeit slowly. This was something that she had been unable to do following the stroke. By the grace of God, she was beginning to experience healing in her body, with sensations starting to seep back into her left arm.

Within a few moments, though, as she lay in the intensive-care ward, intubated and hooked up to incessantly beeping medical equipment, her left arm started to tremble with strain.

"Don't worry about praying for a breakthrough," I assured Heather. Smiling at her, I gestured to one of my pastors who was with me and told her, "Leave the praying to us."

Then, tapping my index finger on the side of my head, I told her, "But watch your mental movies. Make sure that you play the right movies in your mind."

What did I mean by that? I was telling her to see what God sees and ignore all the *sounds, scents, and sights that her natural senses were picking up in the hospital environment.* I was encouraging her to fill her mind with mental images of herself being healthy, strong, and basking in the love of her family at home. I didn't want her to keep seeing all the worst-case scenarios in her mind.

Then I said to her, "It takes a thought to heal a thought."

It was a word that I had received in my spirit for her. For some reason, I just felt like the enemy had succeeded in planting a wrong thought or mental

59

picture in her mind, and that had to be removed and replaced with the right thoughts, pictures, and beliefs that are based on the unchanging Word of God. Shortly after our meeting, Heather was discharged from the hospital and her condition improved.

My friend, if you are being tormented by wrong or negative thoughts in your mind, you need the truth of God's Word to uproot them. Keep meditating on God's Word and promises to you. As you do, the negative, defeatist thoughts that have kept you in fear and anxiety will be replaced with God's good thoughts to bless you with peace and wholeness in every area of your life. Let His Word give you a vision of a bright future full of hope and good things!

Today's Thought
*It takes a thought based on God's Word to heal a negative
or defeatist thought.*

Today's Prayer
*Father, thank You for showing me in Your Word today that
You have an awesome plan for my life right now, and for my future.
Let Your Word take root in my heart and mind, and help me see
beyond all that my natural senses are picking up about my situation.
Help me to see what You see and to fill my mind with the truth
of Your Word that uproots all that is wrong and destructive.
I believe that the light of Your Word has the power to expose,
remove, and replace any lie of the enemy, and I
choose to believe Your Word. Amen.*

Today's Reflection on Right Believing

DAY 21

See What God Sees

Today's Scripture

And do not be conformed to this world, but be transformed by the renewing of your mind…

ROMANS 12:2

Learning to see what God sees is a powerful key in right believing. It involves replacing your wrong beliefs with right beliefs based on God's Word. When Jesus saw the man with the withered hand, He didn't just see the withered hand, He saw that there was more than enough grace for that hand to be made completely whole. Jesus said to the man, "Stretch out your hand!" The man did as told, and his hand was completely restored and made as whole as his other hand (see Mark 3:1–5).

Now, you don't say "stretch out your hand" to someone whose hand is obviously shriveled and disabled unless you see differently. Jesus sees differently from you and me. That's why we need to go back to God's Word and learn to see what He sees. When Jesus sees a disease, a lack, or someone trapped in fear, guilt, addiction, and sin, He doesn't just see the problem. He sees God's healing, grace, and power superabounding in that area of weakness.

You too can change what you believe by seeing beyond what your natural eyes see. Press in to see what God sees. In your very area of lack, struggle, or challenge, see His superabounding grace all around your current situation. Jesus says to you today, "My grace is sufficient for you, for My strength is made perfect in weakness" (2 Cor. 12:9). Give all your weaknesses, failings, and mistakes to the Lord Jesus and see Him transform your weaknesses into strengths.

What you believe is powerful, so are you going by what you see or what God sees? You may not be able to stop negative thoughts from passing through your mind or unhealthy emotions such as fear gripping your heart, but you can definitely anchor your thoughts and emotions on the unshakable Word of God. You can certainly ensure that you believe right regarding what God says about you in His Word, which contains His precious promises to you. The more you learn and believe right about His love and what His Word says about your situation and your life, the more your thoughts will line up with His thoughts about you. You'll begin to develop thoughts of peace and not of evil, thoughts of hope and a bright future (see Jer. 29:11). And you'll be transformed!

Today's Thought

In my very area of lack, struggle, or challenge, God's superabounding grace is all around my current situation. I choose to see and believe that His grace is sufficient for me.

Today's Prayer

Lord Jesus, thank You that right in the midst of the lack, struggles, and challenges I'm facing, Your superabounding grace is all around me, forgiving me, healing me, providing for me, and transforming my weaknesses into strengths. Help me to always go to Your Word to see my situation as You see it, and to anchor my thoughts and emotions on Your unshakable Word. I believe that as I choose to believe what Your Word says about me and my situation, You are transforming me from the inside out. Amen.

Today's Reflection on Right Believing

DAY 22

Turn on the Light of God's Word

Today's Scripture

Your word is a lamp to my feet and a light to my path.
PSALM 119:105

D erek is a successful business owner who attends our church regularly and who has an amazing testimony. Before he experienced his breakthrough though, life was harrowing for him. It all started one morning when he read a newspaper article about a man of his age who had suddenly died of a heart attack. Derek couldn't explain it, but from that moment on, it was as if the air started to thin, and he began experiencing respiratory difficulties. Without him knowing it, fear had begun to coil itself around his heart like a python.

Day by day, Derek started to experience all kinds of evil imaginations of himself getting hurt and dying while doing the simplest day-to-day activities. He suffered escalating bouts of debilitating anxiety attacks as fear tightened its grip on his heart. As his mental oppression worsened, and convinced he was severely ill as his breathing difficulties increased, Derek checked himself into a hospital, where he was told his was not a heart problem but an anxiety problem.

That was when Derek was introduced to and began listening to some of my messages over and over again. He told me, "You said to focus on the Word of God and not on my problems. And that was exactly what I did! I began turning away from those dark thoughts and allowing the light of Jesus' words to come into my situation."

Derek's breakthrough began when he turned on the light of God's Word and allowed it to shine upon him and his situation. One of his favorite verses that gave him both courage and comfort was the Lord saying to him, "I will never leave you nor forsake you" (Heb. 13:5). He would speak this verse whenever he was fearful and then tell himself, "The LORD is my helper; I will not fear" (Heb. 13:6).

Equipped with God's Word, Derek began playing the right mental movies in his mind. Every time the anxiety attacks came and the evil imaginations began to replay in his mind, he would wield these Scriptures like a weapon against the onslaught of the serpent's attack. The more he proclaimed, "I will never leave you nor forsake you. The Lord is my helper; I will not fear," the more the grip of the serpent began to loosen and weaken. He found that he could breathe freely again and his heart no longer felt constricted. Strengthened by the Word, he began to see the Lord with him always. He began to see himself full of health and protected from harm. Derek was completely healed and released from all his fears as he began to replace the wrong mental movies that he had been playing in his mind with the right ones.

Beloved, God's thoughts are greater than the devil's thoughts. His light is greater than any darkness. You'll put an end to the enemy's days of using fear to torment you and manipulate your thoughts when you, like Derek, turn on the light of God's Word and allow it to shine upon you and whatever negative situation you may be in. Let His Word anchor you in His love, strengthen your heart, and paint the right pictures for your breakthrough and an amazing future.

Today's Thought

*When I allow the light of God's Word to shine upon me and
my situation, dark thoughts, fears, and evil imaginations
cannot continue to stay in my mind.*

Today's Prayer

*Father, thank You for revealing the power of Your Word to
me today. Thank You for reminding me that You will never leave
me nor forsake me. Thank You that that is the truth no matter
how bad the darkness around me may seem. Your Word is truth and
it is greater than any darkness that may threaten to consume me.
In the days to come, help me grow in the knowledge of Your Word
and what it says about Your love for me. I believe that even now,
the Word that I have just read about You is dispelling every dark
and negative thought in my mind, and putting Your thoughts
and Your pictures of faith in my heart. Amen.*

Today's Reflection on Right Believing

DAY 23

The Power of Redeeming Thoughts

Today's Scripture

Fix your thoughts on what is true, and honorable, and right, and pure, and lovely, and admirable. Think about things that are excellent and worthy of praise.

PHILIPPIANS 4:8 NLT

What mental movies are you playing in your head today? Are they thoughts of defeat and despair or thoughts of victory and favor? Faith is simply saying what God says about you and seeing what God sees in you and your situation.

Remember what I shared in an earlier reading about how it takes a thought to heal a thought? Unlike the world, which teaches you to empty your mind to achieve peace, God's way is to fill your mind with fresh, powerful, and redeeming thoughts.

The apostle Paul tells us, "Fix your thoughts on what is true, and honorable, and right, and pure, and lovely, and admirable. Think about things that are excellent and worthy of praise" (Phil. 4:8 NLT). So it's not just trying to blot out bad thoughts with your willpower. It takes a thought to replace a thought. It takes a right belief to replace a wrong belief. You need God's truth to replace the enemy's lies that have kept you in bondage.

My friend, if a wrong, bad, or negative thought is lodged in your mind today and you can't seem to shake it, stop trying! Perhaps you're lying in a hospital bed and can't help but think of the worst-case scenario. You're attempting to suppress it, but it's not working. Well, stop! Stop trying to erase it from your mind. That just won't work. What you need to do is replace that destructive thought with a thought that's from God. That's the only way to deal with a wrong thought and begin the healing process.

Start to meditate on truths such as, "Surely Jesus has borne my sicknesses and carried my pains. The chastisement for my wholeness fell upon Him, and by His stripes I am healed. With long life He will satisfy me" (see Isa. 53:4–5 and Ps. 91:16). Begin to play mental movies of yourself getting well, being discharged from the hospital, having fun with your kids, or going on a nice holiday!

Today's Thought

*Bad thoughts don't disappear as a result of my willpower.
They disappear when they are replaced with thoughts
that are from God.*

Today's Prayer

*Father, thank You that You haven't left me on my own to somehow
stop all the wrong thoughts and lies the enemy uses to keep me in
bondage. You have given me Your Word and Jesus. Help me fix my
thoughts on Jesus, His grace and His finished work. He is true and
excellent and worthy of all praise. Let Your Word bring healing,
life, and liberty from every wrong belief and bondage as I meditate
on it and Your grace. I believe that as I declare what You say about
me in Your Word and see how You see me and my situation, I will
experience Your unmerited favor and victory. Amen.*

Today's Reflection on Right Believing

DAY 24

How to Be Kept in Perfect Peace

Today's Scripture

You will keep him in perfect peace, whose mind is stayed on You, because he trusts in You.
ISAIAH 26:3

You need the truth of God's Word to uproot any wrong belief. This is why it's so important to get into His Word and take time to meditate upon verses that reveal God's unwavering and unfailing love for you. For instance, if you find your mind drifting into anxious thoughts over the smallest things, I encourage you to memorize and quote today's scripture: "You will keep him in perfect peace, whose mind is stayed on You, because he trusts in You" (Isa. 26:3).

Whenever I feel stressed or worried about something, I pull away from life's hustle and bustle and simply meditate on God's promises. Sometimes I like to drive to a quiet park, and as gentle anointed music plays in my car, I feed on and speak His Word, allowing it to permeate my spirit: "God's Word declares, 'You will keep him in perfect peace, whose mind is stayed on You.'" And I tell the Lord, "Yes, Lord, it is You who will keep me in perfect peace. Perfect peace comes from You. I just need to rest in Your grace and keep my mind on You. I don't need to think about what to do about this challenge. As I trust in You and keep my mind stayed on You, You will lead me and guide me. My trust is not in my own strength, but in You and You alone, Jesus."

What am I doing here? Instead of allowing stress and worry to get to me, I'm training my heart to see how God sees my challenges. The bigger God becomes in my heart, the smaller my challenges become. In fact, many times when I just relax and keep my mind on the Lord, His peace and wisdom begin to flow in me, and the challenge that I was previously so worried about becomes minute and inconsequential in the presence of Almighty God.

Are you faced with an insurmountable circumstance today? Learn to see what God sees by meditating on His Word, and let His peace drive out your anxiety. Let His wisdom direct your paths.

Today's Thought

The bigger God becomes in my heart, the smaller my challenges become. When I keep my mind on the Lord, His peace and wisdom will begin to flow in me and direct me to victory.

Today's Prayer

Father, I choose to keep my eyes on You today. Instead of focusing on how big my challenges are, I choose to see You watching over me, going before me and taking care of all my needs. In the midst of my challenges, I look to You to keep me in perfect peace and to lead me by Your wisdom to do the right thing at the right time. I receive Your perfect peace right now, and I thank You for leading and guiding me in whatever I need to do today. Amen.

Today's Reflection on Right Believing

DAY 25

What God Sees When He Looks at You

Today's Scripture

But he who is joined to the Lord is one spirit with Him.
1 CORINTHIANS 6:17

One of our key ministry partners, Ron, shared how he had a dear friend named Tyler, who was from a good Christian family, was great at sports, and was living the "American Dream." After college, however, Tyler started hanging out with the wrong crowd and developed a severe drug and drinking problem, which in turn led to a series of devastating mistakes. Within a twenty-four-month period, Tyler lost everything he held dear in his life. Ashamed and miserable, Tyler dropped out of church and almost gave up on life, God, and grace. But God, in His grace, was still reaching out to Tyler (through Ron), as Ron related in this story:

> *One night, while jogging at a park and listening to a message by Pastor Prince, I felt God prompting me to send Tyler a text message. I felt that God wanted me to ask Tyler, "What does God see when He looks at you?" So while running, I texted him exactly those words. After a long time, I received his text reply:*
>
> *Tyler: "Are you serious?"*
> *Ron: "Yes."*
> *Tyler: "Well…I'm sure it's not good."*
> *Ron: "Jesus."*
> *Tyler: "What do you mean?"*
> *Ron: "I mean, when God looks at you, He sees Jesus!"*
> *Thirty minutes later, I got this message:*
> *Tyler: "Thanks, man, you don't know how badly I needed to hear that!"*

Would it bless your heart to know that this is the very message God wants you to receive today? If you are like Tyler, then you believe God's love for you depends on your actions. You honestly believe God is ashamed of you because of your mistakes and failures. Well, you may have either not heard or have forgotten that the payment for your sins has already been made in full upon the body of Jesus at the cross. Therefore, when God looks at you today, He doesn't judge, esteem, and measure you according to your imperfections. He sees you in the Beloved—He sees you in Christ, and He sees the blood that has been shed for you by His dear Son.

When God looks at you today, He sees Jesus. Because of this, His thoughts toward you are thoughts of loving-kindness, forgiveness, blessings, and favor. Jesus paid an immensely heavy price on the cross so that you can live life completely accepted and unconditionally loved by God. Knowing and believing this will make all the difference in how you live your life—no matter what is staring you in the face.

Today's Thought
When God looks at me today, He sees me in Christ. He does not see my imperfections, but sees His Son's blood, and therefore accepts me completely and loves me unconditionally.

Today's Prayer
Father, thank You that on the cross Jesus paid the heavy price for my sins, failures, and shame. Open the eyes of my heart, Lord, to see what You see—that I am in the Beloved, in Jesus, and that His blood covers me completely. I receive Your loving-kindness, forgiveness, blessings, and favor. Today, I choose to stand tall, believing that because of Jesus, I am completely accepted and unconditionally loved by You. Amen.

Today's Reflection on Right Believing

DAY 26

What Actually Happened at the Cross?

Today's Scripture

For He made Him who knew no sin to be sin for us, that we might become the righteousness of God in Him.

2 CORINTHIANS 5:21

Once, the Lord showed me a vision of what happened at the cross. I saw how all the sins of the entire human race (lies, deceit, envy, bitterness, adultery, addiction, bondage, murder) and all the consequences of sin (fear, sicknesses, guilt, disease, and condemnation) swirled around Jesus like evil spirits and demons, laughing heinously, taunting and tormenting Him. Jesus became like a magnet for all sin and of His own volition accepted all this sin into His own body.

You and I will never be able to imagine the excruciating pain that tore through His body at the cross. Every malignant cancer, every tumor, every sickness, and every disease came upon Him at the same time. He who knew no sin took upon Himself the mountainous weight of all men's darkest and foulest sins. He took it all Himself.

The Word says that "He Himself took our infirmities and bore our sicknesses" (Matt. 8:17). "Himself"—a singular, reflexive pronoun that signifies the exclusion of you and me. Since He Himself has taken the full punishment, judgment, and condemnation for all sin, you and I are excluded from every punishment, judgment, and condemnation for all sin when we receive Him as our Savior.

But the story did not end there. Jesus did not die on the cross in the middle of receiving upon Himself all of humanity's sins. He took it all and accepted it all in His body. Then the fire of God's judgment was unleashed upon His own precious Son, and only when every last sin had been punished did Jesus cry out, "IT IS FINISHED!" moments before breathing His last breath (see John 19:30). Can you see that? Jesus held on at the cross until every single sin that you have ever committed and will ever commit was punished in His own body. That is why we call what Jesus has accomplished at the cross a "finished work."

Now, what is your part today? Your part is to believe with your heart and confess with your mouth that Jesus Christ is the Lord of your life and that all your sins have been paid for at the cross. If you believe that all your sins have been forgiven, sin will have no more power over you. You don't have to walk around with "a mountain of sin" on your shoulders anymore because this "mountain of sin" was laid squarely on the shoulders of another—Jesus. He Himself has already paid the price for your sins, so stop condemning yourself!

Today's Thought

Because Jesus Himself has already paid the price for my sins,
I can stop condemning myself.

Today's Prayer

Lord Jesus, because You love me, You went to the cross and
suffered for me. Thank You for taking the weight of all my sins
and bearing the punishment for every last sin until You completely
exhausted God's wrath against my sins. I believe that because of
Your finished work, I stand completely forgiven, with every sin
paid for and with the right to live free from condemnation today.
As I look to You to help me live by this truth every day, I believe
that sin will no longer have dominion over me. Thank You
for Your amazing grace, Lord Jesus. Amen.

Today's Reflection on Right Believing

DAY 27

Only Believe

Today's Scripture

*"And as Moses lifted up the serpent in the wilderness,
even so must the Son of Man be lifted up, that whoever believes
in Him should not perish but have eternal life."*
JOHN 3:14–15

Do you know why Jesus chose the cross? He went to the cross so that whoever believes in Him can receive the gift of eternal life.

Whoever *believes*. That is all you need to do to step into the inheritance that was purchased for you with the blood of the Son of God. Believe in HIM. Believe in Jesus. Believe in what He has done for you at the cross. Believe that all your sins have been imputed to Him and all His righteousness has been imputed to you (see 2 Cor. 5:21). Believe in the divine exchange. Believe in His love. Believe that all your sins have been punished at the cross and that through Jesus you have received the gifts of righteousness and eternal life.

Look at John 3:15 again. Tell me, who qualifies for salvation? The Word of God doesn't say, "Whoever obeys Him perfectly and keeps all His commandments." It doesn't say, "Whoever never fails again." It simply says, "Whoever *believes* in Him." Whoever believes in Him will not perish but have eternal life. The only action needed on your part is to believe!

Pastor Prince, how can simply believing in Jesus make me righteous? There must be something more that I must do to earn and deserve God's love for me.

Don't write it off just because it sounds simple, and don't underestimate the power of right believing. When you believe right—when you believe that you are made righteous through Jesus—you will end up producing the fruits of righteousness. The apostle Paul refers to "the fruits of righteousness" in Philippians 1:11, and he specifies that they are "by Jesus Christ." When you set your eyes on Jesus and Jesus alone as the source of your righteousness and forgiveness, you will end up producing the fruits of righteousness, holiness, and moral character.

Indeed, the Bible tells us it is when we don't see or have forgotten that we have been cleansed from our old sins that we end up lacking in self-control, godliness, and brotherly love (see 2 Pet. 1:5–9). Can you see how when you believe right, you will end up living right? So make Jesus, His forgiveness, and His love the center of every part of your life!

Today's Thought
When I make Jesus, His forgiveness, and His love the center of every part of my life every day, I will end up living right!

Today's Prayer
Lord Jesus, thank You for the gift of eternal life. I can never praise You enough for choosing the cross for me and for redeeming me with Your precious blood. I believe in You. I believe that all my sins have been imputed to You and all Your righteousness has been imputed to me. And I believe that when I set my eyes on You and You alone as my righteousness, I will end up producing the fruits of righteousness, holiness, and moral character. Amen.

Today's Reflection on Right Believing

DAY 28

The Gracious Gift of Righteousness

Today's Scripture

For if by the one man's offense death reigned through the one, much more those who receive abundance of grace and of the gift of righteousness will reign in life through the One, Jesus Christ.
ROMANS 5:17

If you struggle, as many believers do, with whether *you* deserve to be blessed, favored, and victorious, you are asking the wrong question.

The question you should be asking is, does *Jesus* deserve to be blessed, favored, and victorious? Because you are in Christ, having a blessed future is not contingent on how much you strive to be perfect or how hard you work at changing yourself. It is contingent on the person of Jesus.

The Bible proclaims, "as He is, so are we in this world" (1 John 4:17). Does Jesus deserve to be blessed, favored, and victorious? Then so do you! This is what being in Christ Jesus means. It means that today, God assesses you and sees you based on the perfection of Jesus Christ. Jesus' righteousness is your righteousness. In fact, the Bible explains that because Jesus, who knew no sin, became sin for us, we are now the righteousness of God in Christ (see 2 Cor. 5:21).

"Righteousness" is a legal term. It means to have right standing before God. *Vine's Expository Dictionary of Biblical Words* defines righteousness as "that gracious gift of God to men whereby all who believe on the Lord Jesus Christ are brought into right relationship with God."[2] In other words, your right standing before God is based upon Jesus' right standing before God.

Today, you are as righteous as Jesus because your righteousness is from Him. He purchased it for you at the cross. When you received Him as your Lord and Savior, He took away all your unrighteousness once and for all and gave you *His* gift of righteousness. This righteousness is something that you can never obtain or achieve through your right doing; it can only be *received* by your right believing in Jesus.

And do you know what happens when you receive this gift of righteousness? The Bible declares that "those who receive abundance of grace and of the gift of righteousness will reign in life through the One, Jesus Christ" (Rom. 5:17). Hey, when you reign, your addictions don't. When you reign, sicknesses don't. When you reign, fear, depression, and every obstacle that is obstructing you from living your life to the fullest will be torn down and flushed out!

Today's Thought

Today, I am as righteous as Jesus because the righteousness I have is His own righteousness given to me as a gift.

Today's Prayer

Father, thank You for Your abundant grace and gift of righteousness. Because of Jesus' perfect work at the cross, You see and assess me based on His perfection. You see me clothed in Jesus' righteousness and You bless me with what Jesus deserves. Help me to keep growing in the revelation of how my righteousness is a gift from You that can never be earned. I believe that as I keep receiving Your grace and gift of righteousness, You will cause me to reign over every challenge and bondage in my life. Amen.

Today's Reflection on Right Believing

DAY 29

See Who You Really Are

Today's Scripture

...to the praise of the glory of His grace, by which
He made us accepted in the Beloved.
EPHESIANS 1:6

N ancy, who lives in Texas, discovered my ministry via television and began to have a personal revelation of God's goodness and how righteous she was through Christ's finished work. Writing to me about how God's grace has not just impacted her life but the lives of her entire family, she shared:

> When I first saw you on television five years ago, I was rather skeptical. However, something about you was different. I knew in my spirit that you were teaching the true gospel. So I began watching your sermons every day, sometimes twice a day. The more I watched, the more I saw the wisdom of God on you, and the more I wanted to have a relationship with God and Jesus.
>
> At that time, I was at a low point in my life and I was about to give up on my marriage. I was even questioning my faith and God. I didn't realize how much I'd kept God in a box and only involved Him in certain areas of my life because I thought He was judging me.
>
> When I finally heard the truth about the gospel, I ran with it! Never will I look back because you have taught me the true freedom that Jesus died to give me. Praise God! Once the veil was removed, I realized how righteous I really am, and God just started blessing my socks off!
>
> My marriage has turned around and is now growing stronger. We're going on the twelfth year in our marriage, and I thank God for the four beautiful and healthy daughters He has blessed me with. God has also promoted my husband in his career and given him a salary increase. In addition, God has recently upgraded us to an amazing neighborhood and even opened the doors to a charter school for two of my girls. He has given us so much favor because at least five hundred people are on the waiting list for this school!

And that's not all. About a year ago, when I was watching you teach in Israel, I told the Lord quietly in my heart, "Lord, I want to go to Israel. I don't know how I ever will, but I want it." I never thought about the trip again until early April this year when God dropped a free trip to Israel into my lap and opened every door for me to go!

My heavenly Father has shown me that I am His daughter and that He is willing to take care of every need for the rest of my life! I did nothing to deserve it! My light is shining, and everybody wants to know what it's all about.

Today, when you look into the mirror, what do you see? Do you see yourself trapped in all your failings, mistakes, and sins? Or do you see what God sees?

My dear friend, when God sees you today, He sees Jesus. Use your eyes of faith and believe that as Jesus is, so are you. In God's eyes, you are accepted, you are righteous, you are favored, you are blessed, and you are healed. You are freed from all sin, all pangs of guilt, all forms of condemnation, and from every bondage of addiction! See yourself as God sees you and begin to experience His freedom and victory in every area of life.

Today's Thought

In God's eyes, I am righteous, I am favored,
I am blessed, and I am healed.

Today's Prayer

Father, thank You for Your Word that tells me I am accepted in
Christ, the Beloved. I believe that as Jesus is beloved, righteous,
favored, and full of health, strength, and wisdom, so am I today.
I believe that as Jesus is free from, and high above, every disease,
depression, and addiction, so is Your grace and goodness causing me
to walk in the same freedom and power in every aspect of my life.
Thank You, Father, for Your grace toward me. Amen.

Today's Reflection on Right Believing

DAY 30

Irreversibly Blessed

Today's Scripture

"Behold, I have received a command to bless;
He has blessed, and I cannot reverse it."

NUMBERS 23:20

Take time to reread today's scripture. They are precious words, and they reveal how God sees you and me today. They were spoken by a prophet named Balaam, who had been hired by Balak, the king of Moab, to invoke a curse to drive his enemy, the Israelites, from his territory. However, when Balaam opened his mouth to curse, blessings from God flowed out upon the Israelites instead (see Num. 23:21–24)!

Do you know that when God blesses you, no one—no prophet, no sorcerer, and no devil—can reverse it? You are irreversibly blessed! You can never be cursed! No generational curse or any other curse can come upon you because God has already blessed you! That includes being redeemed from the curse of the law as recorded in Galatians 3:13: "Christ has redeemed us from the curse of the law, having become a curse for us (for it is written, 'Cursed is everyone who hangs on a tree')."

When your enemies say negative things about you out of envy, jealousy, and fear, or if there are people spreading nasty lies about you to assassinate your character, know this: the Lord is your defender. It is God who gives influence to words, and He can cause their words to fall to the ground. He can even, as we have just read, turn their curses into blessings. You don't have to get all flustered, agitated, and angry. Just know that the Lord is on your side and that when He has blessed you, no one can reverse it. Amen!

I want this right belief to sink deep into your heart: *in Christ Jesus, you are irreversibly blessed.* No matter how dire your circumstances may seem right now, put a smile on your face and a spring in your step. Whom the Lord has blessed, no one can curse! God is going to see you through this difficult patch. Things are going to turn around for your good. You don't have to live in disappointment, discouragement, and despair. As you can see in the biblical account of Balaam, if God is on your side, who can be against you?

Today's Thought

In Christ Jesus, I am irreversibly blessed.

Today's Prayer

*Father, thank You that in Christ Jesus I am blessed and no
one and nothing can reverse this. Your Word says that Jesus has
redeemed me from every curse including generational curses, so I
don't have to live life afraid of bad things that may happen to me.
I can live life with boldness and freedom from fear. Because You are
for me, I also don't have to be afraid of what others say about me.
You will even turn others' curses into blessings. Thank You
for putting strength in my heart through Your Word and for
showing me Your grace today. Amen.*

Today's Reflection on Right Believing

DAY 31

What God Doesn't See

Today's Scripture

*"He has not observed iniquity in Jacob, nor has
He seen wickedness in Israel."*

NUMBERS 23:21

Today's scripture is part of the irreversible blessing we read about yesterday that God placed in Balaam's mouth. It gives us even more reason to rejoice as we learn to see what God sees. Take a closer look at what God says in the verse above and just pause for a moment. Was there iniquity in Israel? (When God used the word "Jacob" here, He was referring to all the children of Israel.) Was there any sin in Israel? Or was everybody in the encampment perfect?

If you were to zoom in from the top of the mountain into the encampment of Israel, it's not hard to imagine that a wide variety of imperfections, sins, iniquities, and wickedness was present throughout the camp. But the question is, did God see it?

Look at Numbers 23:21 again. Notice that God did not say there was no sin or iniquity in His people. He simply said He did not see it. Similarly, He is not saying that there is no sin in you. What God says is, "I don't see it."

Wait a minute, how can an unbendingly holy God not see sin in me?

My friend, it is because those same holy eyes saw all your sins punished in the body of Jesus Christ. Your sins were punished into nonexistence.

In the Israelite encampment, even though there were iniquities, sins, and wickedness, God did not see any of them because the blood of bulls and goats, which they offered up to the Lord daily, covered the children of Israel. How much more true that is for us today, we who are washed clean forever by the blood of the Lamb of God, Jesus Christ, our beautiful Savior.

Under the old covenant, the Israelites enjoyed a *temporal* covering through the animal sacrifices, but for us, the atonement and payment for all our sins by Jesus Christ is *eternal*. That is why God does not observe sin and iniquity in you nor has He seen wickedness in you. When God looks at you today, He sees you as a righteous, forgiven, healed, favored, blessed, accepted, and beloved son or daughter because of the cross of Jesus.

Now, do you see yourself as God sees you?

Today's Thought

I am washed clean forever by the blood of the Lamb of God, Jesus Christ, my beautiful Savior.

Today's Prayer

Father, thank You that my sins were punished into nonexistence in the body of Jesus Christ. Thank You that I have been washed clean forever by the blood of the Lamb of God. I believe that You see me as Your beloved child today, righteous, forgiven, healed, favored, blessed, and accepted. Thank You for eradicating every wrong belief I have about You and how You see me, through the light of Your Word. Amen.

Today's Reflection on Right Believing

DAY 32

The Key to Faith

Today's Scripture

...fixing our eyes on Jesus, the author and perfecter of faith,
who for the joy set before Him endured the cross, despising the
shame, and has sat down at the right hand of the throne of God.
HEBREWS 12:2 NASB

As humans, not only do we have a propensity to zoom in on every little flaw in our physical and emotional makeup, but we also have a tendency to know, remember, and replay in our minds the sins, failings, and mistakes we have made. We condemn ourselves for even our smallest flaws instead of focusing on how God really sees us—perfect in Christ.

This is why it takes faith to believe that God sees you righteous. It takes faith to believe that He does not see you in your sins, that He does not observe sin or iniquity in you. It takes faith to believe that He means what He says when He says, "For I will be merciful to their unrighteousness, and their sins and their lawless deeds I will remember no more" (Heb. 8:12). It takes faith to believe that God will not remember your failings and mistakes!

But Pastor Prince, my sins are staring right at me. How can I have faith to believe that God doesn't see them?

My friend, the key to faith is found in looking to the source of faith—Jesus. As the Bible says, "fixing our eyes on Jesus, the author and perfecter of faith" (Heb. 12:2 NASB). Your faith to believe is found in Jesus! The Amplified Bible puts it this way: "Looking away [from all that will distract] to Jesus, Who is the Leader *and* the Source of our faith [giving the first incentive for our belief] and is also its Finisher [bringing it to maturity and perfection]."

In other words, turn your eyes away from your own flaws, imperfections, failings, and mistakes, and just fix your eyes on Jesus. The more you see Jesus and His finished work, the more faith arises in your heart to believe that all your sins are truly forgiven. You can start on a clean slate and have a brand-new beginning in Christ. The old is gone, and the new has come!

Today's Thought

The key to faith is found in looking to the source of my faith—Jesus.

Today's Prayer

Lord Jesus, I turn my eyes away from my flaws, imperfections, failings, and mistakes, and just fix my eyes on You. Thank You for Your unchanging promise that You will not remember my failings and mistakes. Because of Your finished work, I am free to start on a clean slate and receive Your fresh mercies every day. Amen.

Today's Reflection on Right Believing

DAY 33

From Glory to Glory

Today's Scripture

But we all, with unveiled face, beholding as in a mirror the glory of the Lord, are being transformed into the same image from glory to glory, just as by the Spirit of the Lord.
2 CORINTHIANS 3:18

I believe that Jesus is doing a great work in your life right now. Maybe you can't see it because there's something that you have done in your past that you just can't seem to shake off, that seems like weights around your feet holding you down. Beloved, today is the day for your breakthrough. Learn to see what God sees by fixing your eyes on Jesus.

You need to understand that what you see or how others see you is not as important as how God sees you. Many people think that God sees them in their sins and is just waiting to pounce on them to punish them. This wrong belief produces wrong living. If you see God this way, you can't help but be in constant fear, insecurity, and anxiety over your past sins. Today, make a decision to turn your eyes to Jesus, for He has already made you, the believer, righteous with His blood!

In fact, the more you behold Jesus, the more you are transformed "from glory to glory, just as by the Spirit of the Lord" (2 Cor. 3:18). Fixing your eyes on Jesus is the greatest holiness. Many think they have to *do more* in order to be more holy, accepted, and loved by God. The truth is, when you behold Jesus more and see His love, His forgiveness, His abundant grace, and His gift of righteousness purchased for you with His own blood, you will be transformed supernaturally.

Holiness is a by-product of seeing Jesus in His grace. When you see Jesus and receive His love and grace every day, your heart is transformed inwardly. This is not outward behavior modification. This is real change that is sustained by a heart touched by His grace and by an emancipated conscience that is forever freed from guilt. This is when that addiction begins to drop from your life. This is when that fear begins to dissolve in His perfect love, and that condemnation arising from your past mistakes is cleansed by His precious blood.

What a life! This is the life that God wants you to experience. Can you see it? Can you see what He sees?

Today's Thought
The more I behold Jesus in His grace, the more I am transformed from glory to glory.

Today's Prayer
Father, thank You for the glorious, abundant life You want me to experience every day! Through Your Word, I want to behold more and more of Jesus. I ask You to keep showing me more and more of Your Son, His grace, and His beauty. I believe that as I fix my eyes on Jesus, I will be transformed from glory to glory by Your Spirit. Amen.

Today's Reflection on Right Believing

DAY 34

Precious in God's Eyes

Today's Scripture

*"He who overcomes shall be clothed in white garments,
and I will not blot out his name from the Book of Life; but I will
confess his name before My Father and before His angels."*

REVELATION 3:5

I want to show you another aspect of how God sees you today through a beautiful truth about the breastplate of the high priest of ancient Israel. Today, Jesus is our High Priest, and as we examine the breastplate, I want you to see something powerful about the way the Lord sees His people.

Notice in the illustration that there are twelve stones on the high priest's breastplate, and the names of the twelve tribes of Israel are engraved on the stones. For example, "Judah" is engraved on the sardius stone set in the first row, and "Gad" is engraved on the diamond set in the second row.

These twelve stones represent God's people today. Notice how God depicts His people, you and me, as precious stones. He didn't use common rocks and pebbles. He deliberately chose very costly, rare, and precious gems such as sapphire, topaz, emerald, amethyst, diamond, onyx, and jasper to represent you and me (see Exod. 39:9–14). Also, of all the garments donned by the high priest, the breastplate is closest to the heart. This speaks of how much the Lord values you and His desire to keep you close to His heart. In His eyes, you are very costly, precious, and loved.

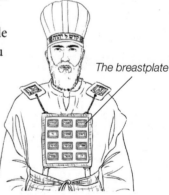

The breastplate

*The high priest of Israel:
The names of the 12 tribes
of Israel are engraved on
12 precious stones found
on his breastplate.*

Notice also that the names of the tribes of Israel were not merely written on the gems; they were *engraved* (see Exod. 39:14). This means that once you

100 DAYS *of* RIGHT BELIEVING

become a believer in Jesus, your name is forever engraved in His Book of Life. If your name were only written, you might think that it could easily be erased or blotted out. But the truth is that Jesus has *engraved* your name on a precious stone, and He keeps it close to His heart.

Can your name ever be blotted out of its place on God's heart? Just look at what Jesus promises those who are born again: "He who overcomes shall be clothed in white garments, and I will not blot out his name from the Book of Life; but I will confess his name before My Father and before His angels" (Rev. 3:5). Beloved, through Christ Jesus, you are an overcomer, and in Christ Jesus, you are eternally secure. Rest in the assurance that your name will not be blotted out from the Book of Life. It will remain engraved on stone and close to God's heart for all eternity!

Today's Thought

*In Jesus' eyes, I am very costly, precious, and loved.
I am eternally secure because Jesus has engraved my name
forever in His Book of Life.*

Today's Prayer

*Father, thank You that in Your eyes, I am very precious, costly,
and greatly loved. Thank You for showing me how closely You hold
me to Your heart. I believe that You have engraved my name in Your
Book of Life, and I rest in the deep assurance that my name will
never be blotted out from it. I am eternally secure! Amen.*

Today's Reflection on Right Believing

....

....

....

....

....

....

....

DAY 35

Break the Cycle of Defeat

Today's Scripture

Therefore there is now no condemnation for those who are in Christ Jesus.
ROMANS 8:1 NASB

People who believe erroneously that God is hard on them for their failures will inevitably be hard on the people around them, and most of all, they will end up being really hard on themselves. They cannot forgive themselves for the mistakes they've made in the past and end up punishing themselves, whether they know it or not. It's a vicious cycle of defeat. The more they can't forgive themselves, the more they hurt themselves with all kinds of behaviors and the more they end up bound by various destructive addictions. This leads to even more guilt, which in turn drives them to punish themselves even more—and the cycle continues.

I believe the root cause of many sinful habits, fears, and addictions can be traced to condemnation. I want to talk to you today about going after condemnation as the root to help you receive God's forgiveness in those areas so that you can break out of your cycle of defeat and step into a new cycle of victory.

Are you living with some unresolved guilt and condemnation today? I have great news for you. When you realize that God's heart is not in condemnation but in forgiveness, your entire life can be turned around for His glory! I have personally witnessed so many lives transformed when they just take a small step of faith to believe in His grace and receive His forgiveness in their lives.

Instead of punishing themselves for their mistakes and disqualifying themselves, these people began to correct their beliefs and receive God's forgiveness by seeing Jesus taking on their punishment. They began to see their Savior qualifying them to receive every blessing from God for their marriages, families, and careers.

Right now I want to encourage you to release the built-up guilt and condemnation for whatever mistakes you've made over the years to the Lord.

Would you pray today's prayer with me? It's a simple but powerful prayer. I encourage you to pray this prayer every time you fail and experience guilt and condemnation in your heart. Stop punishing yourself—your answer is found at the cross of Jesus. I promise you that when you turn to Jesus and remind yourself just how forgiven and righteous you are in Christ every time you fall short, you will start living like the forgiven and righteous person Jesus has made you.

Today's Thought
God's heart is not in condemning me but in forgiving me.

Today's Prayer
Lord Jesus, I don't want to live under guilt and condemnation anymore. Today, I release all my failings, sins, and mistakes into Your loving hands. And I receive Your forgiveness right now into my heart. Thank You for Your precious blood that washes me whiter than snow. Right now I stand in Your righteousness, favor, joy, and peace. Amen!

Today's Reflection on Right Believing

DAY 36

God Loves You Perfectly

Today's Scripture

But God demonstrates His own love toward us, in that
while we were still sinners, Christ died for us. Much more then,
having now been justified by His blood, we shall be saved
from wrath through Him.
ROMANS 5:8–9

God is a God of forgiveness. He knows you perfectly and still loves you perfectly. We are slaves to the idea that if someone sees our flaws, they won't love us anymore. Well, while that may be true in human relationships, God is not like that.

God sees all our imperfections, failings, and flaws on Jesus at the cross. Our sins and ugliness do not turn Him off. In fact, to Him they are occasions to demonstrate His grace and forgiveness through the blood of His Son, who has removed all our sins efficaciously at Calvary.

So don't be embarrassed about your flaws, mistakes, and imperfections. God knows your weaknesses better than you do, and He loves you just the same. His Word reminds us that Jesus is not someone "who cannot sympathize with our weaknesses." Instead, Jesus was tempted in all points, yet He was without sin (Heb. 4:15). He understands every temptation and every trial that you are going through. He is not disappointed with you, and He is not waiting for you to live up to a set of dos and don'ts before He forgives and loves you. The Bible says, "But God demonstrates His own love toward us, in that while we were still sinners, Christ died for us. Much more then, having now been justified by His blood, we shall be saved from wrath through Him" (Rom. 5:8–9).

Did you get that? *When* did God love you?

That's right, *when you were still a sinner*. Before you even knew Him, when you were still in sin, He already loved you. How much more today, when you have been cleansed by Jesus' blood and made righteous! Having received Jesus' righteousness, you are righteous forever. Even when you fall into sin, your sins don't make you a sinner again.

When you fall short today, you are still the righteousness of God. This is because your righteousness comes from Jesus. In the same way that a beautiful butterfly cannot morph back into a caterpillar, once you have been made righteous by the blood of Jesus, you cannot morph back into a sinner. Knowing your righteous identity in Him then gives you the power to overcome every sin, every addiction, and every bad habit!

Today's Thought
God knows me perfectly and still loves me perfectly.

Today's Prayer
Father, thank You for demonstrating Your love toward me, in that while I was still a sinner, You sent Jesus to die for me. Thank You that though You know my every flaw and failing, You still love me perfectly. Despite my imperfections, You still see me righteous today because of Jesus. Today, I believe that through Your gift of righteousness, I have the power to overcome every sin, every addiction, and every bad habit in my life. Amen.

Today's Reflection on Right Believing

DAY 37

Sweet, Sweet Grace

Today's Scripture

*For sin shall not have dominion over you, for you
are not under law but under grace.*
ROMANS 6:14

In many places today, all you hear is more teaching on right doing, right doing, and more right doing! But I believe what we need is more teaching on right *believing*. What we need to do is keep pointing people to Jesus, His grace, His finished work, and His forgiveness. I have no doubt then that their right believing will produce right living. They will become people whose hope is not in the righteousness *they* can produce, but in the *gift of righteousness* from Jesus Christ and what *Jesus* can produce in them.

Let me share with you a testimony I received from Lucas that demonstrates this truth:

Even though I was raised in a Christian home with parents who are both totally dedicated to Jesus, I fell into drug abuse. I tried attending church, but listening to the sermons made me feel like I just couldn't confess my sins enough, repent enough, or hate my sins enough to get God's forgiveness.

Then one day a very dear friend gave me a copy of your book, Destined To Reign. *The book rocked my spiritual world. I saw that sin was not the issue. The issue was not understanding the grace of my wonderful Lord and Savior. When I saw the finished work of Jesus, I realized that God is not up there with a big stick waiting for me to mess up so that He can beat me with it.*

As I continued reading your book and feeding on the gospel of grace, I was set free from a five-year drug addiction in just five days! And I know it's all through the sweet, sweet grace of Jesus being revealed in my life.

Thank you, Pastor Prince, for your book, resources, and sermons. I want to know this God of grace more, and I want my family to also know

Him as a God of grace and not a God of law who condemns His children. I have never known a loving God as I do right now!

Can you see how powerful living with a consciousness of Jesus' forgiveness can be? Sin has no dominion over your life when you are under grace. Sin cannot take root in your life when you are established in God's forgiveness. Receiving His forgiveness and gift of righteousness puts you in a cycle of victory over sin, whereas those who receive condemnation for every wrong thought in their mind enter into a never-ending cycle of defeat. Do you see the difference?

Today's Thought

Sin has no dominion over my life when I am under grace.

Today's Prayer

Father, thank You for unveiling to me the sweet, sweet grace of Jesus and the gift of righteousness that is mine through His finished work. I receive Your forgiveness into my heart today, and I thank You that as I live conscious of Your grace in my life, sin shall have no dominion over me. Amen.

Today's Reflection on Right Believing

DAY 38

The Unforced Rhythms of Grace

Today's Scripture

"Are you tired? Worn out? Burned out on religion?
Come to me. Get away with me and you'll recover your life. I'll show
you how to take a real rest. Walk with me and work with me—
watch how I do it. Learn the unforced rhythms of grace. I won't
lay anything heavy or ill-fitting on you. Keep company with
me and you'll learn to live freely and lightly."
MATTHEW 11:28–30 THE MESSAGE

Do you feel as though you are trapped on a never-ending treadmill based on your own efforts to try to earn God's forgiveness, God's approval, and God's acceptance? That is Christian religion. If you are trying to earn your own forgiveness and thinking that God is constantly mad at you, I am here to tell you that is not the heart of God.

When Jesus spoke of "the unforced rhythms of grace," He means that there is an ease and enjoyment when you walk in His grace. This is in contrast to the struggle and strain found in self-effort. There is such rest when you know there is nothing you can do to earn His forgiveness. Give up on your own self-righteousness, which the Bible describes as "filthy rags" (Isa. 64:6), and with open arms and an open heart, receive His forgiveness!

The key to getting out of a cycle of sin and defeat is to receive and to stop beating yourself up. Receive and stop punishing yourself because your sins have already been punished on the body of another—His name is Jesus, our beautiful Lord and Savior. No wonder the gospel is called the *good news.*

When you understand God's grace and forgiveness, you will understand the difference between obligation and relationship. Under the old covenant of the law, right living is done out of religious obligation. Under the new covenant of grace, every thing we do today is birthed out of an inward motivation that flows directly from a love relationship with Jesus.

My friend, God is not a legalist. He doesn't want you to read His Word just because He said so, as a religious obligation. He wants you to experience His love and spend time in His Word because you *want to* enjoy His sweet presence. You can read His Word out of legalism and to try to earn God's forgiveness and acceptance, or you can do it out of relationship because you know you have been forgiven. The reality is, when you don't read the Bible, you should not be feeling guilty; you should be feeling hungry.

Jesus invites you to experience "the unforced rhythms of grace." Keep company with Him and you'll learn to live freely and lightly!

Today's Thought
Jesus invites me to step out of the struggle and strain of self-effort into the unforced rhythms of grace.

Today's Prayer
Lord Jesus, thank You for Your gracious invitation to learn the unforced rhythms of grace. Help me to see when I am slipping into religious obligation, because I want to respond to You out of love and relationship. I believe as I keep company with You and enjoy Your sweet presence that I will know Your heart and Your ways and live in victory. Amen.

Today's Reflection on Right Believing

DAY 39

Be Forgiveness-Conscious

Today's Scripture

*Bless the LORD, O my soul, and forget not all His benefits:
who forgives all your iniquities, who heals all your diseases,
who redeems your life from destruction, who crowns you
with lovingkindness and tender mercies.*
PSALM 103:2–4

Not too long ago, I was driving out for lunch with my wife, Wendy, and for some reason, every time she made a passing comment, I found myself snapping irritably at her or making an unnecessarily provocative remark. Have you had one of those days?

When I reflected on why I was so irritable, I realized it was because I was actually feeling guilty about a couple of matters from earlier in the day. I hadn't necessarily done anything wrong, but I'd just allowed a little bit of guilt to creep into my heart and unconsciously allowed condemnation to come in.

My friend, when you are walking under a cloud of judgment, you can become a really unpleasant person to be around. Trust me, I know what I am talking about. Even if you are an author of books about God's grace and forgiveness, there can be moments where condemnation creeps into your heart and you are completely oblivious to it.

I thank God that when Wendy asked me if there was a reason for my irritability, He gave me that moment of clarity where I could see the condition of my heart. And praise Jesus for a discerning and perceptive wife who didn't take my remarks personally and knew something was not right with me. I remember telling her to let me know the next time she noticed such behavior from me, because it's so easy to slip into condemnation and guilt.

When you're under guilt and condemnation, all day long you can feel lousy, and all your answers have a sting in them. That's not the abundant life, and you know what it all comes back to? It comes back to having a constant sense of God's forgiveness over your life. Instead of taking in and harboring all the guilt, condemnation, and judgment, we need to stand secure in our perfect forgiveness in Jesus.

There is a redeeming quality to being forgiveness-conscious, as opposed to being conscious of your failings, sins, and mistakes. When you are forgiveness-conscious and see your failings on the cross of Jesus, you receive power to break out of your irritability, impatience, and short-temperedness with others. You receive power to break out of your eating disorders, addictions, and anxieties! When you realize that we don't deserve God's forgiveness and grace yet He gives it to us anyway, this revelation of His unmerited favor changes us from within. It dissolves the knots of anger and impatience in us that have built up over the years and frees us to enjoy God's love and to show it to others!

Today's Thought
When I realize that I don't deserve God's forgiveness and grace yet He gives it to me anyway, this revelation of God's unmerited favor changes me from within.

Today's Prayer
Father, thank You that You have secured my perfect forgiveness in Jesus. I believe Jesus bore every one of my failings at the cross, and I receive Your forgiveness afresh today. When I begin to take in and harbor guilt and condemnation, help me to have a constant sense of Your grace, Your unmerited favor. I believe in the redeeming power of Your forgiveness to break out of all that holds me back from experiencing the abundant life that is found in Jesus. Amen.

Today's Reflection on Right Believing

DAY 40

Free and Undeserved

Today's Scripture

And since it is through God's kindness, then it is not by their good works. For in that case, God's grace would not be what it really is—free and undeserved.

ROMANS 11:6 NLT

I love the apostle Paul's description of God's grace: *free* and *undeserved*! When you truly experience this free and undeserved favor and love from God, you don't have to worry about performing. His love and unmerited favor within you will flush out all the wrong thinking and wrong believing, and you will produce good works—true fruits of righteousness that are lasting, sustainable, and enduring!

You may have heard a teaching going around where grace is defined as "divine empowerment." Be careful about defining grace as merely empowerment—that is diluting and reducing what grace truly is.

Grace produces divine empowerment, but in and of itself, the essence of grace is His undeserved, unmerited, and unearned favor. When are you in your most undeserving state? When you have failed. Unmerited favor means that when you have failed and are in your most undeserving state, you *can* receive Jesus' favor, blessings, love, and perfect acceptance in your life. Let me tell you, when you understand and receive grace as God's unmerited favor, not only will you be empowered, you will be healed, and you will be changed from the inside out.

The real danger with defining grace as just divine empowerment is that we can unconsciously flip grace around and instead of seeing it as God's work in our life, we make it our work. From being centered on what Jesus has done, the erroneous definition of grace as "empowerment" swings it to being about what *you* must do and how *you* must perform now that you have received this grace, this "divine empowerment." Can you see this? With such a definition of grace, the onus to live the Christ life falls back squarely on your shoulders.

My friend, make sure that what you believe in your heart always points you back to Jesus and Jesus alone and not to yourself. Remember, it is all

116

about His work, His doing, His performance, and His love in our lives. It never points back to you. Don't be hoodwinked by those who move away from the pristine definition of grace as God's unmerited favor and end up making it all about you and what you need to do. That's not grace. Grace is God's doing—from inception and all the way to the end.

Today, receive His abundant grace—see that God has already started a good work in your life and He alone will lead you to and give you the victory in your area of need.

Today's Thought

Grace is God's doing—His work, His performance, and His love in my life—from inception and all the way to the end.

Today's Prayer

Father, thank You for Your grace—Your free, undeserved favor and love for me. It's not about my trying, my doing, or my performing. I freely receive Your grace—Your favor, love and blessings for every area of need today. I am blessed because of Jesus and Jesus alone— His work, His doing, His performance, and His love in my life— from beginning and all the way to the end. Amen.

Today's Reflection on Right Believing

DAY 41

Effortless Change

Today's Scripture

"Abide in Me, and I in you. As the branch cannot bear fruit of itself, unless it abides in the vine, neither can you, unless you abide in Me. I am the vine, you are the branches. He who abides in Me, and I in him, bears much fruit; for without Me you can do nothing."
JOHN 15:4–5

I'd like you to picture a strong and healthy tree. A strong and healthy tree does not worry about producing fruit or getting rid of the dead leaves on it. As long as it receives the right amount of sunshine, water, and nutrients, it will have healthy sap flowing in it that is brimming with all the right nutrients and that naturally pushes out all the dead leaves. And as long as its inward life—its healthy sap life—keeps flowing, new leaves will spring forth on this tree and good fruits will naturally grow and flourish on all the branches.

My friend, as you begin to receive the sunshine of God's favor and take in the water of His Word, as you begin to feed on Jesus' forgiveness in your life and your righteous standing in Christ, the dead leaves of guilt, fear, addictions, and every type of disorder will begin to be pushed out by the new life of Jesus within you. The transformation you will experience, when it is not based on your own discipline and self-control, is truly effortless. It is no longer, "How will I overcome this anger problem?" or "How will I beat this cigarette addiction?" or "How can I curb this habit of overeating when I am stressed and insecure?" Instead, it becomes, "How will *Jesus* in me overcome this anger problem, this cigarette addiction, this habit of overeating?"

The fruits of your success will be effortless. One by one, the addictions, dysfunctions, and negative emotions will begin to drop off from your life like dead leaves, and new leaves (new positive thoughts and attitudes), new flowers (new desires and dreams), and new fruit (new behaviors and habits) will begin to flourish in your life.

Jesus' word to you today is simply to "abide in Me," and you will bear much fruit.

Today's Thought

As I begin to receive the sunshine of God's favor and take in the water of His Word, as I begin to feed on Jesus' forgiveness in my life and my righteous standing in Christ, the dead leaves of guilt, fear, addictions, and every type of disorder will begin to be pushed out by the new life of Jesus within me.

Today's Prayer

Lord Jesus, thank You that I am a branch in Your great vine and that all I have to do is abide in You. I acknowledge that apart from You, I can do nothing, and that all I need for life and victory flows from You to me. I believe that the fruits of my success will be effortless as I simply receive and feed on Your grace for me every day. Amen.

Today's Reflection on Right Believing

DAY 42

Your Ledger Is Clean

Today's Scripture

*"I—yes, I alone—will blot out your sins for my own sake
and will never think of them again."*
ISAIAH 43:25 NLT

It's so important that you understand, believe, and abide in the truth of God's unmerited favor and forgiveness in your life, even when your behavior is not perfect. Why? Because it frees you to enjoy your relationship with God, to enjoy spending time with Him, and to expect good from Him. It frees you to enjoy peace and rest, good relationships with others, a life of wholeness, and to confidently expect a bright future.

Imagine for a moment that you are a businessperson. Through some bad decisions and some things beyond your control, your business got into serious debt. You've made a habit of avoiding your company's ledger because when you open it, all you're going to see is red, which is a screaming reminder of how much you owe and how unhealthy your business is. You can't help thinking about the ledger, but the more you think of it, the more it fills you with dread.

In the same way, if you keep believing and thinking that there is still unsettled debt between you and God, you can't breathe easy. You become consumed with thoughts of how to pay off your debt. In fact, just the thought of red in your ledger makes you afraid to go to Him or expect His help for anything.

But say a good friend finds out about your business debt, and of his own free will and out of his own pocket, he pays off the debt. Furthermore, knowing that you can't ever pay this debt on your own, he doesn't want you to even try to pay him back. Now (after you've gotten over this incredible news), you're not afraid of your ledger anymore. You can throw off your despair and laugh and look forward to life again. Rather than fear the ledger, you're quite happy to look at your ledger because it declares you are now debt-free and how good your benefactor is.

My friend, this is what Jesus has done for you, and much more. You are perfectly forgiven and righteous through Jesus' finished work. Being the Son of God, He is an overpayment for your sins. And He didn't just cleanse you of your entire life of sins, but He also gave you His very own righteousness and favor. Why? So that you can be free to enjoy being with God and receive all His blessings, with no more consciousness of debt standing in the way. You can live life with a confident expectation of good. There is no red in your ledger (see Col. 2:13–14).

Once in a while, though, because of the force of habit or doubt, you may wake up fearful that you're back in debt. But all you have to do is open your ledger and look at it. It will show you how debt-free you really are, no matter what you feel. Similarly, should you ever experience days when you doubt that God has forgiven you, all you have to do is open the Word of God and see in it how the price has been fully paid, the judgment executed, and every bit of condemnation already meted out on the body of Christ!

Today's Thought

There is no red in my ledger because Jesus has cleansed me of my entire life of sins and given me His own righteousness. Today I can freely receive all of God's blessings with no more consciousness of debt standing in the way.

Today's Prayer

Lord Jesus, thank You that nothing can change the fact that You didn't just cleanse me of my entire life of sins, but You also gave me Your very own righteousness and favor. I believe that You have blotted out every sin and that the ledger of my life has been cleared of all my debts. Thank You for setting me free by Your grace to enjoy Your favor, peace, and abundant life. Amen.

Today's Reflection on Right Believing

DAY 43

Fresh Grace for Every Failing

Today's Scripture

The faithful love of the LORD never ends!
His mercies never cease. Great is his faithfulness;
his mercies begin afresh each morning.
LAMENTATIONS 3:22–23 NLT

My friend, here's some more *good news*: every time you fail, there is fresh grace from Jesus to rescue you. Every time you fall short, confess your righteousness in Jesus by faith. I know you probably won't *feel* particularly righteous, and that is why you need to say it by faith.

I have received so many testimonies of breakthroughs from people around the world who, even as they succumb to their addictions, would confess, "Even right now, I am the righteousness of God in Christ" and eventually found freedom from their bondages. It could be a smoking addiction or an alcohol or pornography addiction. Michael, a brother in Australia, happily shared, "I have just given up smoking by following what you've taught in your books and DVDs (about being conscious of and confessing my righteousness in Christ) whenever I was tempted to smoke. I have also been set free from twenty years of drug and alcohol abuse and am free of paranoid thoughts. I couldn't give them up through my own efforts, but through Christ I have."

The more these people confessed and saw themselves as righteous in Jesus, even in the midst of their failings, the more they came to see their true identity in Christ. The dead leaves began to fall, and they came to the place where they didn't have any desire to ever smoke another cigarette, drink another drop of alcohol, or visit another pornographic website. New leaves, new flowers, and new fruits unconsciously and effortlessly sprang up in their lives. Grace put an end to the barrenness and torment of winter and ushered in perpetual spring for them.

Beloved, if you are grappling with something right now, stop struggling and start receiving. Start receiving the abundance of the Lord's unmerited favor. Start receiving the free gift of His righteousness. Start receiving the cleansing power of His forgiveness. There is nothing for you to do but to soak it all up and to allow His resurrection power to drive out every symptom of death and decay in your circumstances and in your life.

Can I give you an assignment today? Every time you fail, come into God's presence and pray today's prayer. His grace will lift you up!

Today's Thought

Every time I fail, there is fresh grace from Jesus to rescue me.

Today's Prayer

Father, thank You that even right now, Your total forgiveness and Your perfect love are raining all over me because of Your Son's finished work in my life. Take away every lingering sense of ugliness, guilt, and condemnation in me. I believe with all my heart that right now when You look at me, You see me in Christ Jesus. I am clothed in His robe of righteousness, favor, and blessings. Thank You for Your abundance of grace and Your gift of righteousness in my life. Through Jesus, I will reign in this life over every sin, addiction, and failure. Amen.

Today's Reflection on Right Believing

DAY 44

"Neither Do I Condemn You"

Today's Scripture

When Jesus had raised Himself up and saw no one but the woman,
He said to her, "Woman, where are those accusers of yours? Has
no one condemned you?" She said, "No one, Lord." And Jesus said
to her, "Neither do I condemn you; go and sin no more."
JOHN 8:10–11

Dragged into the temple precinct like a rag doll, the woman caught in adultery (see John 8) knew there was no escape. Gloating silently, the mob of religious Pharisees threw her before the feet of a man they called Teacher. Surely, she thought, this man was the religious judge who would officially sentence her to death.

Her merciless accusers fired the first salvo: "Teacher, this woman was caught in adultery, in the very act. Now Moses, in the law, commanded us that such should be stoned. But what do You say?" (John 8:4–5). Anticipating further humiliation, she waited, but heard nothing except a deafening silence. Then, from the corner of her eye, she saw that the teacher had stooped down and was writing with His finger on the ground, with the Pharisees poised around her with rocks in their hands.

Then the teacher stood up before them, and she heard a voice so resounding with majesty that her breath caught in her throat. Articulating each word with a perfect blend of authority and compassion, He declared, "He who is without sin among you, let him throw a stone at her first" (John 8:7). And then He stooped to the ground once more and resumed writing as though the leaders of the synagogue were not even there.

His words bewildered her. Who *was* this teacher? Why was He defending her, a sinful woman and an adulteress? Was *this* the man from the small village of Nazareth who heals the blind and makes the lame walk again? The man whom they say hates legalism and loves sinners? As these questions whirled around in her frightened mind, she heard the sound of her salvation as the rocks that would have battered her to death fell impotent to the ground. One by one, her accusers turned and moved away.

After some time, all she could see were the teacher's sandals. He lifted her head, and she saw His face for the first time. It was a face of compassion and love. A face that glowed with acceptance and assurance. She let her pent-up tears flow as He asked her, "Woman, where are those accusers of yours? Has no one condemned you?" (John 8:10). Throughout her ordeal, no one had spoken to her. *She* had not mattered to her accusers. But now the man who had rescued her was speaking to her and looking at her as if she *mattered*.

Gratefully, she breathed, "No one, Lord!" She knew beyond a doubt that this teacher was no ordinary teacher. That is why she addressed Him as "Lord" and not "teacher" as the Pharisees did. He *was* the Jesus everyone was talking about. Then she heard the words that she would never forget for the rest of her life: "Neither do I condemn you; go and sin no more" (John 8:11).

This Jesus, who saved her life from condemnation and death, is your Savior today. Let the words He said to the woman—"Neither do I condemn you"—ring in your heart today and give you the power to overcome every sin and struggle in your life.

Today's Thought

No matter what I've done, no matter what happens, Jesus does not condemn me because He was condemned in my place at the cross. He forgives me and empowers me to "sin no more."

Today's Prayer

Lord Jesus, You are so worthy of my worship, so great a Savior are You! Thank You for taking my condemnation at the cross so that I can freely receive Your gift of no condemnation and be empowered to sin no more. I believe that no matter what happens, no matter what I've done, You do not condemn me, but You love me and freely forgive me. I choose to live by this truth and by Your words of assurance today. Amen!

Today's Reflection on Right Believing

DAY 45

"No Condemnation" Comes First

Today's Scripture

"For God did not send His Son into the world to condemn the world, but that the world through Him might be saved."
JOHN 3:17

Yesterday's account of the woman caught in adultery demonstrates something very important. What enables someone to have the power to overcome sin? The threat of the law obviously didn't stop the woman from committing adultery. But receiving Jesus' acceptance—knowing that even though she deserved to be stoned to death, He did not condemn her—*that* gave her the power to "go and sin no more."

Notice that Jesus saved the woman righteously. He didn't say, "Don't stone her. Show mercy to her." What He said was, "Let he who is without sin cast the first stone." And on their own accord, the Pharisees and religious mob all left.

Notice also that Jesus did not ask the woman, "Why did you sin?" No, what He asked was, "Has no one condemned you?" It seems as if Jesus was more preoccupied with the *condemnation* of the sin than the sin itself. He made sure that she walked away not feeling the condemnation and shame. Let's not reverse God's order. When God says something comes first, it must come first. God says "no condemnation" comes first, and then you can "go and sin no more."

Christian religion has it in reverse. We say, "Go and sin no more first, then we won't condemn you." What we need to understand is that when there is no condemnation, people are empowered to live victorious lives, lives that glorify Jesus. Grace produces an effortless empowerment through the revelation of no condemnation. It is unmerited and completely undeserved. But we can receive it—this gift of no condemnation—because Jesus paid for it at the cross.

Truth be told, none of us could have cast the first stone. We have all sinned and fallen short. In Christ, we are all on equal ground. If a brother or sister gets tangled in sin, our place is not to judge them, but to restore them by pointing them to the forgiveness and gift of no condemnation that are found in Jesus.

The only person who is without sin and who could have exercised judicial punishment on the woman was Jesus, and He did not. Jesus was in the flesh to represent what was in God's heart. It wasn't judgment. His heart is unveiled in His grace and His forgiveness. I like to say it this way when describing what happened as the Pharisees waited to stone the woman: The Pharisees *would* if they *could*, but they could not. Jesus could if He *would*, but He *would* not. That's our Jesus!

Today's Thought

God's heart is unveiled in His grace and His forgiveness.

Today's Prayer

Father, thank You that what Jesus did at the cross for me is so much greater and more wonderful than what I can ever imagine. Thank You for the gift of no condemnation and for Your undeserved favor because Jesus paid for it all at the cross. I believe that Your grace and forgiveness will empower me to live a life that glorifies You today. Amen.

Today's Reflection on Right Believing

DAY 46

God's Perfect Law Perfectly Fulfilled

Today's Scripture

And you, being dead in your trespasses and the uncircumcision of your flesh, He has made alive together with Him, having forgiven you all trespasses, having wiped out the handwriting of requirements that was against us, which was contrary to us. And He has taken it out of the way, having nailed it to the cross.
COLOSSIANS 2:13–14

Over the past two days, we have considered the account of the woman caught in adultery. Interestingly, the Bible is silent on what Jesus wrote on the ground with His finger. But I believe that when He stooped down, He was writing the Law of Moses. I have been to Jerusalem many times. During one of my visits many years ago to the temple precinct where Jesus would have met this woman, the Lord opened my eyes to see that the floor of the temple precinct was made of hard cobblestone. This means Jesus was not writing on soil. He was writing with His finger on stone.

Then, in a flash, I saw that Jesus was writing *the law* on stone. He was effectively saying to the Pharisees, "You presume to teach Me about the Law of Moses? I am He who wrote the law." Jesus wrote twice on the ground with His finger, thus completing the typology, as we know that God wrote the Ten Commandments with His finger twice.

The first set of the Ten Commandments was destroyed by Moses when he saw the Israelites worshiping the golden calf at the foot of Mount Sinai. God then wrote another set on stones and gave it to Moses for it to be placed under the mercy seat in the ark of the covenant. I had never heard anyone preach this before—it was a fresh revelation straight from heaven. I love it when the Lord opens my eyes to see His grace!

Do you know why it's so exciting to know what Jesus wrote on the ground that day? It's so significant because it shows us that the very author of God's perfect law does not use the law to judge and condemn us today. And it's not because God simply decided to be merciful on us. No! It's because Jesus Himself fulfilled all the righteous requirements of the law on our behalf and took upon Himself every curse and stroke of punishment for our sins on His own body at the cross. We are forgiven because He was judged. We are accepted because He was condemned!

Whatever your challenge today, your answer is found in receiving a fresh revelation of how much you are forgiven in Christ.

Today's Thought

I am forgiven because Jesus was judged. I am accepted because He was condemned.

Today's Prayer

Lord Jesus, thank You for fulfilling all the righteous requirements of the law on my behalf, taking every curse and stroke of punishment for my sins on Your body at the cross. Thank You that You do not use the law to judge and condemn me today. I believe that I am forgiven and accepted because You were judged and condemned in my place. Amen.

Today's Reflection on Right Believing

DAY 47

Forgiveness and Healing Go Hand in Hand

Today's Scripture

But He was wounded for our transgressions, He was bruised
for our iniquities; the chastisement for our peace was upon Him,
and by His stripes we are healed.
Isaiah 53:5

There is another reason we can rejoice in the knowledge that Jesus has borne the punishment that was due us: forgiveness and healing go hand in hand. The Bible says that He who never broke a single law of God "...was wounded for our transgressions, He was bruised for our iniquities; the chastisement for our peace was upon Him, and by His stripes we are healed" (Isa. 53:5). Do you see how healing and the price for our forgiveness are so closely intertwined in God's Word?

Many today are struggling to heal themselves from their sicknesses, diseases, mental dysfunctions, and addictions. I want to announce to you today that our part is to *receive* forgiveness from Jesus and to believe that we are forgiven every single day. The more forgiveness-conscious we are, the more easily we will experience healing and liberty from every bodily ailment, mental oppression, and destructive habit.

One of my favorite psalms goes like this: "Bless the Lord, O my soul; and all that is within me, bless His holy name! Bless the Lord, O my soul, and forget not all His benefits: Who forgives all your iniquities, who heals all your diseases" (Ps. 103:1–3). Now which comes first? The consciousness that all your sins are forgiven precedes the healing of all your diseases!

And the operative word here is *all*. Some of us are comfortable with receiving partial forgiveness in certain areas of our lives. But we refuse to allow Jesus' forgiveness to touch some dark areas—areas that we can't let go of and that we can't forgive ourselves for. Whatever those mistakes may be, I encourage you to allow Jesus to forgive you of *all* your sins and receive healing for *all* your diseases.

136

My friend, let the past go. Let the mistakes go. Allow yourself to be free, and learn to forgive yourself by receiving with an open heart Jesus' total and complete forgiveness today.

Today's Thought
I believe Jesus forgives me of all my sins, and I receive His divine healing for my mind, emotions, and body.

Today's Prayer
Father, thank You that Your Word is so clear about all that Jesus accomplished on the cross on my behalf. Your eternal Word states that by the stripes of Jesus, I am healed, and that peace is mine because of His sacrifice. May all that is within me bless Your holy name! I open my heart and receive Jesus' total and complete forgiveness and healing for all my diseases. Amen.

Today's Reflection on Right Believing

DAY 48

What This World Is Hungry for

Today's Scripture

But if the Spirit of Him who raised Jesus from the dead dwells in you, He who raised Christ from the dead will also give life to your mortal bodies through His Spirit who dwells in you.
ROMANS 8:11

I want to share with you a wonderful praise report from Pat, who lives in Ohio and wrote me this email:

> *Amazing changes in my life have started ever since I fed on the truths you taught. I now have a joy and appreciation for life that I never had since my teen years (and I am in my fifties). I have a permeating peace that manifests in every area of my life—from parenting to my finances to my health.*
>
> *Initially, when I started listening to you, I did not believe what you taught regarding holiness, fullness of blessings, and righteousness through faith in the finished work of Christ. When I got sick and bedridden, I continued to watch you as I was unable to do more. You supported your teachings with Scriptures, and I began to realize your teaching was true. I began to read the Gospels and epistles with an enlightened mind and could clearly see that you were presenting the gospel.*
>
> *Once I embraced these truths, my physical condition began to change. I had been suffering from a spinal cord and disc injury for which there was no cure. Spine specialists refused to operate on me unless I came to the stage when part of my body became paralyzed, which is the usual course of events. I had been in a state of pain and was physically incapacitated for more than two years.*
>
> *Since feeding on your teachings, I have regained use of my body and most of the previously excruciating pain has subsided. Now I am able to relax and be confident and trust in the willingness and availability of*

the power and grace of God to heal me. This came as a result of increased faith, the elimination of condemnation, an understanding of the Holy Communion, and an increased awareness of God's love for me.

I have also been freed from a ten-year habit of smoking cigarettes. I used to only smoke at night just before going to bed in order to calm my nerves. I tried for years to break the habit but could not. I always felt so guilty for having such a weakness. But once I realized that God did not hold my weakness against me and that He accepted me unconditionally and would still bless me, I let go of all the worry and struggle over my habit and I began to experience peace and rest.

A few months later, I was able to quit smoking. It's as if the habit was effortlessly removed from my life, like it just dropped off me. I know that it was the Spirit of God working in me to perfect me and give me the power to no longer crave for cigarettes.

Truly, my life has been transformed. The gospel is what this world is hungry for and much in need of. I have been a believer for more than twenty-five years and have never heard it presented the way you teach it. Keep awakening the world to the love and grace of God, as well as the hope of salvation, blessing, and glory in Christ Jesus!

Dear reader, you too can experience this victory. The more you let the waterfall of God's forgiveness and unmerited favor wash over you every day, the more you'll receive His health for your body and soundness for your mind. Now begin to enjoy His love and let His grace work in you and for you, to bring you to a place of greater health, emotional strength, peace, and enjoyment in life.

Today's Thought

It is God's grace working in me that brings me to a place of greater health, emotional strength, peace, and enjoyment in life.

Today's Prayer

Thank You, Jesus, for loving me. Today I receive Your complete forgiveness in my life, and I forgive myself for all my sins, mistakes, and failings. I release them all into Your loving hands. I declare that in You, I am completely forgiven, free, accepted, favored, righteous, blessed, and healed from every sickness and disease. Amen!

Today's Reflection on Right Believing

DAY 49

Win the Battle for Your Mind

Today's Scripture

For as he thinks within himself, so he is.
PROVERBS 23:7 NASB

I want you to be aware that as you begin practicing some of the keys that we have been discussing, you'll experience some battles in your mind that will challenge your beliefs. Be encouraged to know that you don't have to be afraid of these battles. Jesus said, "And you shall know the truth, and the truth shall make you free" (John 8:32). Based on God's Word, right believing is the key that unlocks the treasures of God in your life, giving you *access* to the fullness of His love, grace, favor, blessings, and forgiveness. Jesus has already paid the price on Calvary's hill. The hindrance then between you and your victory is your wrong beliefs. The battle has to do with your beliefs.

The enemy knows that if he can control your thought life, he can manipulate your emotions and feelings. For instance, if he can make you entertain thoughts of guilt, failure, and defeat, you will begin to feel lousy about yourself, physically weak, and even depressed.

Our emotions are flags that indicate to us what our thoughts are. Thank God for emotions. They tell us if something is terribly wrong with our thoughts. Many of us are not cognizant when our thinking slides down a slippery slope to fear, doubt, pessimism, and anxiety. However, God has designed us in such a way that we can quickly recognize our thinking through our emotions. Try this: whenever you begin to sense negative emotions, such as fear, worry, guilt, and anger, stop and ask yourself, "What am I thinking?"

Your emotions follow quickly at the heels of your thoughts. If your thoughts are negative, you will naturally produce negative emotions. Conversely, if your thoughts are positive in Christ, you will produce positive emotions.

That is why there is a battle for your mind. The devil wants to keep your thoughts negative so that he can keep you defeated. He is a master of mind games, and he doesn't play fair. When he first tempted Adam and Eve in the garden, he made them doubt God's motives by insinuating that God was deliberately withholding something good from them, when in reality God was protecting them. The devil's strategy hasn't changed—he is still using fears, lies, accusations, guilt, and condemnation to ensnare believers today and to make them doubt God's perfect love, forgiveness, and superabounding grace.

My friend, are there areas you are fearful and anxious about today? Realize that those fears and anxieties indicate the presence of wrong beliefs in your life that God wants you to be freed from. Replace those wrong beliefs with right beliefs based on God's Word, and you will eradicate those fears and anxieties. Through the power of right believing, you will win the battle for your mind.

Today's Thought
Right beliefs and thinking positive thoughts in Christ will launch me toward my breakthrough.

Today's Prayer
Father, thank You for the emotions that indicate what my thoughts are and warn me when my thinking is sliding down a slippery slope to fear, worry, guilt, and anger. Help me to be aware of the battle that is going on in my mind and to be able to see through the enemy's lies, accusations, guilt, and condemnation that would ensnare me. I declare that through the power of right believing in Your love and what Your Son, Jesus, has done for me, I will win the battle for my mind. Amen.

Today's Reflection on Right Believing

....

....

....

....

....

DAY 50

Jesus Is Greater

Today's Scripture

...He who is in you is greater than he who is in the world.
1 JOHN 4:4

Beloved, there may be a devil out there who tries to drag you down in defeat, but the Bible tells us clearly that we have One greater than he inside of us. It is important that you be established in this truth. You don't have to be afraid of the devil, because Jesus, who is in you, is greater than the devil in this world. No matter what the enemy's evil tactics are, he will not prevail against you in this battle. The devil is a defeated foe. Greater is He who is in you than all the negative thoughts the enemy can throw at you. Greater is He who is in you than the feelings of guilt and inadequacy. Greater is He who is in you than every accusation that is leveled against you.

Stand strong on this declaration: "No weapon formed against you shall prosper, and every tongue which rises against you in judgment you shall condemn" (Isa. 54:17). Wow! No weapon formed against you shall prosper. The Bible doesn't say that you will not experience any challenges or be faced with any attacks. But it does promise that you can be confident in the certainty that they shall not prosper against you.

Do you know why you can stand firm on this promise today? In the very same verse, God goes on to declare that "This is the heritage of the servants of the LORD, and their righteousness is from Me" (Isa. 54:17). This protection is your heritage. God does not protect you because of your right doing; He protects you because your righteousness is from the Lord Himself!

Notice that the weapon that is against you could have *already been formed*, which means that it may already have been conceived, prepared, and aimed at you. Don't be afraid. Whatever this weapon or challenge may be, know beyond any doubt that it shall not prevail against you. This is God's promise to you today—*no weapon formed against you shall prosper*. Not because your behavior is perfect, but because your standing in Christ is perfect. Your victory is firmly secured through Jesus' finished work, which is your heritage in Christ.

Today's Thought
No weapon formed against me shall prosper because my standing in Christ is perfect.

Today's Prayer
Lord Jesus, I stand on the great truth that You live in me and that You are greater than the devil in this world. I stand on the great truth that my righteousness is from You. Therefore, I believe that when trials and attacks come, no weapon formed against me shall prosper and my victory is secure. Amen.

Today's Reflection on Right Believing

DAY 51

Pulling Down Strongholds

Today's Scripture

*For though we walk in the flesh, we do not war according to
the flesh. For the weapons of our warfare are not carnal but
mighty in God for pulling down strongholds…*

2 CORINTHIANS 10:3–4

As you meditate on Bible promises that proclaim God's truth over your life, you are already beginning to win the battle for your mind. It's not a coincidence that Jesus was crucified on Golgotha, which actually means "Place of a Skull" (Matt. 27:33). Your breakthrough has to begin in your mind first.

This battle for your mind is not waged externally. Our weapons in this battle are not physical or tangible. Our weapons are the weapons of right believing, and they are mighty in God for pulling down strongholds that have kept us bound. These are strongholds that can only be utterly torn down by rightly believing in the truth of God's Word.

The devil can only sow wrong thoughts in your mind, but he cannot control what you believe! When you start to believe right, every lie and wrong thought will melt away like butter on a hot, sunny day. Lies can imprison and defeat you only to the degree that you don't allow God's truth to come into your situation to liberate you. Listen closely to what Jesus said: "If you abide in My word, you are My disciples indeed. And you shall know the truth, and the truth shall make you free" (John 8:31–32). What this means is that whatever stronghold you are trapped in today, truth from Jesus will set you free!

Strongholds are wrong thoughts and lies that have been perpetuated in your mind over weeks, months, or even years. These entrenched wrong beliefs cause you to live in bondage to addictions and in a state of fear, guilt, anxiety, or chronic depression.

God's Word tells us in no uncertain terms that the warfare takes place in our minds and is won by us "pulling down strongholds, casting down arguments and every high thing that exalts itself against the knowledge of God" (2 Cor. 10:4–5). The place where the enemy launches his attacks against you is in your thoughts and imagination. I believe that once you are aware that there is a war for your mind, and that it is between wrong beliefs and right beliefs, you have already won half the battle! Keep hearing, keep believing, and keep renewing your mind with the truth of God's grace and love for you. And whatever stronghold you may be trapped in today, the truth from His Word will set you free!

Today's Thought
The weapons of right believing are mighty in God for pulling down strongholds that have kept me bound.

Today's Prayer
Father, thank You for giving me mighty weapons that pull down the enemy's strongholds as I rightly believe in the truth of Your Word. Open my eyes to see the truth of Your grace that sets me free and let Your Word take root in my heart and mind. I believe that even the entrenched wrong beliefs that have caused me to live in bondage will be utterly torn down, and I will be liberated in Jesus' name. Amen.

Today's Reflection on Right Believing

DAY 52

Anchor Your Identity in Christ

Today's Scripture

Yet in all these things we are more than conquerors
through Him who loved us.
ROMANS 8:37

Several years ago, I preached a message on how the devil sometimes uses the first-person pronoun to plant thoughts in our heads to deceive us. For example, he doesn't say, "You have an eating disorder" or "You have an addiction." The devil uses the first-person pronoun to sow thoughts such as these in your mind: "*I* have an eating disorder" or "*I* am addicted to pornography." He makes you think that you are thinking those thoughts of defeat. He wants you to believe that is who you are.

Upon hearing this message, a man named Walter, whom the devil had used this strategy on and trapped in a destructive addiction for many years, went home after church, locked himself in his room, and for the first time declared out loud, "I am not an addict!" He chose to reject this evil mind-set in the name of Jesus. He related this: "At that very moment, I felt something powerful happen inside me. I don't know how to describe this. It was as if life became spectacular because of the love of God, and I couldn't contain the feeling."

After making that confession out loud, Walter said, "My addiction stopped. I just lost all interest, and I don't feel even a little bit tempted. All the wrong desires are gone, and best of all, I know I love Jesus more than ever before and I can't live without Him. I am renewed. I am reborn. I know that everything is in His control, and I am blessed and forgiven."

Wow! What an amazing testimony of God's power and goodness in this brother's life. With just one declaration, he broke the mental stronghold that the devil had placed him under for many years. That is truly the power of right believing. If you can change what you believe, you can change your life, just like this brother did.

Are there lies about your identity that you believe in today? Break the power of those lies by declaring your identity in Christ. Say out loud, "I am a child of God. I am healed, forgiven, righteous, and holy in Christ Jesus." Instead of believing the devil's lies when he uses the first-person pronoun strategy against you, speak your true identity in Jesus.

———————————

Today's Thought

I can break the power of lies about who I am by declaring my identity in Christ.

Today's Prayer

Father, thank You that one declaration of truth about who I really am in Christ has the power to break a stronghold that has held me for years and years. I am declaring my identity in Jesus right now. I am Your child. I belong to Jesus, who bought me at the cost of His life on Calvary. I am healed, forgiven, righteous, and holy in Him. Amen.

Today's Reflection on Right Believing

DAY 53

Bring Every Thought into Captivity

Today's Scripture

...bringing every thought into captivity to the obedience of Christ.
2 CORINTHIANS 10:5

Unfortunately, unbeknownst to many believers today, the enemy has launched malicious disinformation campaigns that have effectively enslaved them for years to low self-esteem, self-hatred, guilt, eating disorders, perversions, inordinate fears, and all kinds of crazy habits and addictions. I want to expose the enemy's lies and to help you see with pristine clarity the enemy's deceptive and manipulative tactics. These lies will collapse like a house of cards the second you see your true identity in Christ.

Your weapons for this warfare are found in the truth of God's Word, and they are mighty and have the power to overthrow and destroy every stronghold that has been built up through disinformation and wrong believing. And the way we can destroy these strongholds in our mind is by "bringing every thought into captivity to the obedience of Christ" (2 Cor. 10:5).

When I was a young believer, I was taught that it was my responsibility to bring my every thought into obedience *to* Christ. I tried and struggled with that for years and ended up with more mental oppression, stress, and guilt than I had started with. One day God opened my eyes and said to me, "Son, keep your focus and your thoughts always on the obedience *of Christ*, and that will be a powerful weapon to pull down the devil's strongholds in your mind." When He said that to me, it felt like the lights were suddenly switched on in my head.

So what does it mean to capture every thought to the obedience of Christ? Simply this: to focus on Jesus' obedience to the Father at the cross, through which we were all made forever righteous the moment we believed in Him. Can you see that our obedience today under the new covenant begins with choosing to *believe* that we are made righteous by *Christ's obedience* at the

153

cross? The apostle Paul describes our obedience as "obedience to the faith" (Rom. 16:26)—believing right about what Jesus has done to make us righteous. And when we believe right like this, we will find His grace motivating and empowering us to think and live right.

God's Word tells us, "The just [righteous] shall live by faith" (Rom. 1:17). You can say it like this: the righteous shall live by right believing. When you have right believing, you release the power of God to live right. The next time you have negative thoughts, catch yourself and look toward the obedience of Christ. See the cross. See Jesus. See Him washing your mind with His precious blood.

When you believe the gospel, the true gospel that says you are righteous through Jesus' obedience (see Rom. 5:19), you will have right living. The right results will follow. My friend, the more you believe right that you have been made righteous and blessed through Christ's obedience, the more you will see the fruit of obedience in your life. Praise Jesus for His marvelous grace!

Today's Thought

Today, I choose to focus on Christ's perfect obedience and how His obedience at Calvary makes me righteous, whole, favored, and complete.

Today's Prayer

Lord Jesus, thank You that it was Your obedience at the cross that makes me righteous. Thank You that as I keep my thoughts focused on Your obedience, You will cause me to live a life of obedience unconsciously. You will cause me to think and live right. I believe that I am righteous, whole, favored, and blessed today through Your obedience alone, and I believe that You are pulling down the enemy's strongholds in my mind as I rest in this truth. Amen.

Today's Reflection on Right Believing

DAY 54

The Enemy's Mind Games

Today's Scripture

*...I fear, lest somehow, as the serpent deceived Eve
by his craftiness, so your minds may be corrupted
from the simplicity that is in Christ.*

2 CORINTHIANS 11:3

The devil loves to play mind games. When I was a young, impressionable believer, I was taught erroneously that a Christian could commit "the unpardonable sin" when he blasphemes against the Holy Spirit (Matt. 12:31–32). Just the thought that I could commit this sin put me under severe oppression. I was really worried that I had already committed the unpardonable sin and was on a one-way ticket to hell. That one thought opened up all kinds of terrible experiences in my life.

What is the "unpardonable sin"? It is simply the sin of an unbeliever continually rejecting Jesus as his or her Savior, as the self-righteous Pharisees were doing in Jesus' day. But it is impossible for a believer to commit this sin, because he or she has *already* received Jesus as his or her Savior as well as been forgiven and pardoned of every sin through His finished work at the cross.

Unfortunately, no one taught me about God's grace then, and I lived under this dark cloud of mental oppression for more than a year before the truth of God's grace set me free. During that time, I kept hearing in my mind, "*I* have committed the unpardonable sin." I would be praying to God, and wrong, sometimes vulgar, thoughts would come in, and my response then typically was, "What is wrong with me? I'm a Christian. I shouldn't be thinking these kinds of thoughts!" At other times, the devil would knock me on the head with accusations such as "How can you think such nasty thoughts and still call yourself a Christian?" The enemy is an expert at throwing thoughts (using the first-person pronoun) into our minds and then backing off and coming at us as a legalist to knock us on the head with the very thoughts that he first put in our heads.

My mental oppression lasted for as long as it did because I always felt that I had to do something about it. I felt responsible for those thoughts in my head, and the moment I believed those horrible thoughts were mine, the devil got me right where he wanted me—defeated, guilty, and feeling condemned. Every major bondage begins in the mind.

How do you win this battle for your mind? My friend, the answer is found in the person of Jesus. He is your righteousness. He is in heaven and He can never be removed, no matter what you have or have not done. Your righteousness is Jesus Christ Himself, and He is the same yesterday, today, and forever (see Heb. 13:8)!

So don't be deceived any longer. The apostle Paul says, "I fear, lest somehow, as the serpent deceived Eve by his craftiness, so your minds may be corrupted from the simplicity that is in Christ" (2 Cor. 11:3). The gospel is simple. It's all about Jesus. It's not about you. Christ is our righteousness, our obedience, our sanctification, and our justification. Glory and boast in Christ and Christ alone. The enemy will try to make it all about you. Keep it simple. Unlike Eve, don't be deceived by his craftiness. Ignore him and simply focus on the simplicity that is in Christ.

Today's Thought
The enemy cannot make inroads into my mind when I simply focus on Jesus as my righteousness and sanctification.

Today's Prayer
Father, thank You that the gospel is simple—it's not about me and what I do or don't do; it's all about Jesus and what He has done for me. Help me to see through all of the enemy's mind games, lies, and distortions of truth that try to keep me bound in legalism. I believe that Jesus alone is my righteousness, my obedience, my sanctification, and my justification. My eyes are fixed on Jesus and my glory and boast are in Christ alone. Amen.

Today's Reflection on Right Believing

DAY 55

Your Breakthrough Is Around the Corner

Today's Scripture

...being confident of this very thing, that He who has begun a good work in you will complete it until the day of Jesus Christ.
PHILIPPIANS 1:6

Several years before my television ministry began broadcasting in America, I received a letter from Max, a United States (US) Navy personnel, who had passed through Singapore and had a life-transforming encounter with the gospel of grace. It contained a beautiful story best told in his own words:

Pastor Prince, I want to share what God has done in my life through my experience in Singapore. I cannot tell you how thankful I am to God that I was miraculously led to your church.

I have been a Christian for about three years, but for well over a year, I was in heavy bondage. Like you, I was convinced that I had committed the unpardonable sin. To me, grace was a bad thing. I knew that I deserved to go to hell under the Old Testament, and because Jesus had come and I still sinned, I felt that I deserved hell all the more. So in my heart, I wished that Jesus had never come. To make a long story short, I got desperate. I was willing to do anything to find peace with God.

Unfortunately, I did not realize that my focusing on doing more for God would only lead me further away from the peace that I so desperately desired. Before long, I became very judgmental. I cut myself off from my Christian friends and even convinced a few that they were on the road to hell with me. I cannot tell you the hopelessness and misery I felt that year. In a journal entry on April 18, 2001, I wrote, "What would I not pay for someone to show me the way to the Lord, not to a religion but to the living God."

Well, I received orders to catch a submarine out to Singapore. The first four days after my arrival in Singapore were spent doing touristy things. One night I went out with all of the officers to a bar. The bar was especially distasteful, and I left early. On my walk back to the hotel, I prayed to the Lord desperately for some fellowship. Then, to my amazement on the busy street, I heard a man ask me, "Are you looking for a church?" Of course I said yes to this man who turned out to be a member of your church. He gave me the directions to the church and told me there was a Bible study service the following day.

When I attended the Friday night Bible study service, I was still really judgmental and questioning everything, but the message was like nothing I had ever heard before. Then on Sunday, I attended your church service and even ordered thirteen of your tapes. I left that day on the submarine, and I listened to Winning the Battle of Your Mind *about eight times in a row!*

My life has never been the same after I caught my first glimpse of God's grace. When I returned to the US after only three weeks on the sub, my mom could see a huge change in my attitude. Where there was once depression, there was joy. Where there was once a judgmental attitude, there was love. Returning to the Naval Academy, I gave the tapes to the friends whom I had convinced were going to hell with me. The next time I saw them, they were full of joy!

I pray that some day I will be able to visit Singapore and your church again. I know Marines are supposed to be tough, but my desire to fellowship with you and your church is so great that it almost brings me to tears. May God's grace and peace be with you and your family.

Interestingly, two years after I received his email, one of the naval officers whom he had given my tapes to actually wrote us to tell us how his own life had also been amazingly changed by the messages. Robby also mentioned that Max had become a well-respected officer in jet pilot training. The love and grace of God had liberated and transformed him into someone who (in Robby's words) "had so much of God's love and joy in him that people just wanted to be around him."

I believe with all my heart that you are next in line to join Max and Robby. Whatever you are in need of—a breakthrough, miracle, healing, restoration, or deliverance—is just around the corner. You may not even be conscious of it, but God has already begun a work in you and He will surely complete it in your life.

There are so many powerful truths in *Winning the Battle of Your Mind*. I would really like to bless you with this message. Books are powerful, but there is something special about listening to the preached Word. If you are interested, please log on to josephprince.com/power to download the free audio message. I believe that this resource will help you to receive a fresh impartation of the Lord's love and grace to win the battle for your mind.

Today's Thought
Whatever I am in need of—a breakthrough, miracle, healing, restoration, or deliverance—is just around the corner.

Today's Prayer
Father, thank You that I have the assurance that the work You have started to do in my life will be brought to completion by Your love and power. By Your grace I will win the battle for my mind. I believe that You are working on my behalf, turning depression into joy, sickness into health, and lack into supply as I rest in Your grace. Amen.

Today's Reflection on Right Believing

DAY 56

Change Your Mind

Today's Scripture

The Lord is not slack concerning His promise, as some count slackness, but is longsuffering toward us, not willing that any should perish but that all should come to repentance.

2 PETER 3:9

The word "repentance" in the New Testament is the Greek word *metanoia*, which simply means "a change of mind." *Meta* means "change" and *noia* refers to your mind. There are religious folks who have this idea that repentance means groveling in dirt and condemning themselves until they feel they have sufficiently earned God's forgiveness.

My question is, how condemned and sorrowful do they need to be before they have genuinely "repented"? And after they have "repented," should they fail again in the same area, does it mean that they did not really "repent" completely the first time? I do not doubt the sincerity of people who believe in "repentance" this way. However, you can be sincere in your intent but still be sincerely wrong when repentance is not based on right believing that leads to inward heart transformation.

It is possible to beat your breast sorrowfully, put on sackcloth and ashes, cry your eyeballs out, and remain unchanged. Sorrow doesn't equal transformation. It is right believing that brings about true repentance (change of mind) and hence genuine transformation. It is impossible to truly repent the Bible way—to experience Jesus, His love, His grace, and His power and to allow Him to change your mind and your belief system—and still remain the same.

Can you see how man-centered teachings on contrition and repentance can sound so good, but in reality trap people in a permanent cycle of defeat and hypocrisy? The truth is, if you are a new creation in Christ, you already hate the sin and the wrongdoing. It vexes your soul, and you are looking for a way out of your bondage. The repentance you need—the change of mind you need—is to know that God has already forgiven you. Stop condemning yourself and walk in His righteous identity to new levels of victory over sin.

Now that you understand what Bible repentance is, let's apply it to winning the battle for your mind. When wrong thoughts come into your head, the repentance or change of mind that you need is to know that those thoughts don't belong to you. Repentance in this situation is not about beating yourself up over those thoughts. I used to do that and it only left me more oppressed and defeated. No, give them no room to flourish by ignoring them while you continue to be established and secure in your identity in Christ. Fill your mind with His thoughts, His living Word, His peace, His joy, and His love.

Today's Thought
Right believing brings about true repentance (change of mind)
and hence genuine transformation.

Today's Prayer
Father, thank You that true repentance simply means a change
of mind that is based on right believing, and this leads to the
transformation of my heart. Thank You for showing me that the
change of heart I need to be free from all bondage is to know that
You have already forgiven me and see me righteous in Christ.
Help me to realize that when wrong thoughts come into my head,
those thoughts don't belong to me. I believe that as I fill my
mind with Your thoughts and living Word, You will help
me to win the battle for my mind. Amen.

Today's Reflection on Right Believing

DAY 57

Always Accepted in Christ

Today's Scripture

"You shall also make a plate of pure gold and engrave on it,
like the engraving of a signet: HOLINESS TO THE LORD....
So it shall be on Aaron's forehead, that Aaron may bear the
iniquity of the holy things...and it shall always be on his forehead,
that they may be accepted before the LORD."
EXODUS 28:36, 38

In the Old Testament, Aaron was the first high priest of Israel. The high priest of Israel is a picture of our Lord Jesus Christ, who is our permanent High Priest today. God instructed that the golden plate of the miter (headdress), which has the Hebrew words *Kadosh Le Yahweh* ("Holiness to the Lord") engraved on it, should always be on the forehead of the high priest so that all Israel would be accepted before God (see the illustration).

What this means is that even when Israel failed in their *thought life*, they were still accepted by God because He judged the nation of Israel based on their high priest. If the high priest was accepted, the entire nation was accepted.

Today we have a perfect High Priest in Christ. It's not your thoughts that qualify you to be accepted by God. Under the new covenant of grace, God is no longer judging you based on your thoughts. God judges you based on His Son. If He is righteous, God sees you as righteous.

Gold plate

The high priest wears a gold plate bearing the words, "Holiness to the Lord" on his forehead.

If He is blessed, God sees you as blessed. If He is under God's unclouded favor, God sees you as under His unclouded favor. If His thoughts are always perfect and filled with holiness unto God, God sees your thoughts as perfect in Christ!

Today when the devil comes to torment your mind, point him to Jesus. Jesus' thoughts are always holy. Remember how the golden plate is always around the forehead of your High Priest and His thoughts are always filled with holiness to God. Look at Exodus 28:38 again: "It shall always be on his forehead, that they may be accepted before the LORD." Therefore, even when your thought life isn't always perfect, know that Jesus' thoughts are *always* perfect. And it's because of His perfection that you are always accepted in Him before God. God will never reject you because your thoughts are imperfect. He is looking at Jesus, and as long as His thoughts are holy, you are accepted!

Today's Thought

When the devil comes to torment my mind, I will simply point him to my representative and High Priest, Jesus, whose thoughts are always holy.

Today's Prayer

Father, thank You that Jesus is my perfect High Priest and that my acceptance with You is based on Him. I acknowledge that my thoughts can waver, but Jesus' thoughts are always perfectly holy. And because He is my permanent High Priest, You will never reject me even when my thoughts are imperfect. I believe that because of Jesus, I am always accepted and approved, and I declare that in Christ I will always win the battle. Amen.

Today's Reflection on Right Believing

DAY 58

Be Strong in the Lord

Today's Scripture

Finally, my brethren, be strong in the Lord and in the power
of His might. Put on the whole armor of God, that you may be
able to stand against the wiles of the devil. For we do not wrestle
against flesh and blood, but against principalities, against powers,
against the rulers of the darkness of this age, against spiritual
hosts of wickedness in the heavenly places.... Stand therefore,
having girded your waist with truth, having put on the breastplate
of righteousness, and having shod your feet with the
preparation of the gospel of peace.
EPHESIANS 6:10–12, 14–15

One of the greatest struggles people face in the battle for their minds is the wrong belief that God is angry with them. The devil knows that if he can cause you to believe that God is mad at you, he can keep you trapped in fear, defeat, and bondage. I want to expose this lie from the devil and show you from God's Word that God is not mad *at you*. He is mad *about* you! God loves you passionately, and He wants you to be fully assured and confident of His love for you.

To be victorious in the battle for your mind, it's important you believe with all your heart that God is for you and not against you. When you use the weapons of right believing to prevail against the wiles of the devil, the Bible calls this being strong in the Lord. Let's go through the whole armor of God (see Eph. 6:10–20) and observe how right believing in all that Jesus has done will always lead us to victory.

The apostle Paul begins with the belt of truth. When the devil comes against you with his lies about you, gird your waist with the belt of truth. The devil cannot deceive you if you are established in what God's Word says about you. He can only make inroads into your mind when you don't know or are unsure about what God's Word says. That's why I encourage people to study God's Word for themselves and to listen to messages that are full of God's grace and truth. Fill your mind and heart with truth and you'll surely defeat the enemy.

Secondly, we already know that the devil will try to attack you with all kinds of accusations and condemning thoughts to make you feel guilty and lousy about yourself. That's why when you are established in the gift of righteousness, his attacks against you will not prevail. All of the devil's fiery darts of accusations are ineffective against the breastplate of righteousness that guards your heart from all fear, guilt, and condemnation.

Now, the enemy will also come in to try to steal the joy you have because of the gospel of peace, which is depicted as shoes here. But when he comes, know and believe that the God of peace will surely crush Satan underneath your feet.

Tomorrow, we'll look at the rest of the armor of God. Rest assured that when you believe right, there is no area of your life in which the devil can prevail against you.

Today's Thought
To be strong in the Lord is to use the weapons of right believing to prevail against the enemy. God is not mad at me, He is mad about me!

Today's Prayer
Father, thank You for providing me with Your armor and the weapons of right believing that help me to stand successfully against the wiles of the devil. Thank You for the belt of truth found in Your Word and for the breastplate of righteousness that guards my heart from all fear, guilt, and condemnation. Thank You for the gospel of peace with which You crush Satan beneath my feet. I believe that You are not mad with me today but You are for me. I choose to live by this truth. I believe that believing right about what Your Word says about me and my situation will always lead me to victory. Amen.

Today's Reflection on Right Believing

....

....

DAY 59

The Whole Armor of God

Today's Scripture

…above all, taking the shield of faith with which you will be able to quench all the fiery darts of the wicked one. And take the helmet of salvation, and the sword of the Spirit, which is the word of God; praying always with all prayer and supplication in the Spirit, being watchful to this end with all perseverance and supplication for all the saints.
EPHESIANS 6:16–18

Yesterday we read about how God has provided us with the spiritual armor of truth, righteousness, and the gospel of peace. Let's continue today with the rest of the armor of God found in Ephesians 6. As we said yesterday, each piece of God's armor is actually a weapon of right believing by which we experience His victory over the devil's mind games. Today let's look first at the piece of armor the Bible calls *the shield of faith* with which to defend yourself and stand strong when the enemy comes against you with thoughts of fear, doubt, and confusion.

In apostle Paul's time, a shield referred to the huge shield that was used by the Romans, which was as big as a door! See your faith as a mighty shield and picture this—as long as your shield of faith is up, you are untouchable. No matter how many fiery darts the devil may pitch at you, ALL of them shall be quenched. Too many Christians are taking up the shield of doubt and quenching the blessings of God instead. Don't let that be you—*face your future with boldness with the mighty shield of faith.*

Another area the devil likes to attack in your mind is the area of your salvation. When you come under attack, apart from the shield of faith, be sure to have on the helmet of salvation. The word "salvation" comes from a beautiful Greek word *soteria*, which definitely includes eternal life, but is an all-encompassing word that means deliverance (from your enemies, diseases, depression, fears, and all evils), preservation, safety, and salvation.[3] So put on the helmet of salvation by meditating on Jesus, and be filled with God's wholeness, protection, healing, and soundness. Let His *soteria* insulate your mind against the enemy's lies.

Lastly, you have also been equipped with the sword of the Spirit, which is the Word of God. Wield the sword of the Spirit by praying in the Spirit and speaking out God's "now word" into your situation. Declare His promises and the truth of His grace over yourself and your circumstances to guard your heart against thoughts of hopelessness, despair and fear.

My friend, the whole armor of God has everything to do with what you believe in Christ. When you believe rightly about His grace and His finished work, every evil strategy the enemy has against you will surely fail. So be strong in the Lord's love for you. Believe that God is for you and not against you. His truth, His righteousness, His faith, His gospel, His salvation, His Word, and His Spirit are all weapons of right believing to overcome all the devil's attacks.

Today's Thought

I choose to believe that God is for me and not against me.
I am equipped with the whole armor of God to face my
future with hope and boldness.

Today's Prayer

Father, thank You that no matter how many fiery darts the
devil may pitch at me, You have given me faith as a mighty shield
to quench them all. By faith I declare that I already have the victory
over every one of the enemy's attacks through Jesus' perfect work
at the cross. I take Your salvation to be all that You mean it to
be—eternal life, deliverance, preservation, and safety. I believe that
blessings are mine because of Jesus and Jesus alone. And I wield the
sword of the Spirit, Your Word, by praying in the Spirit and declaring
Your promises and grace over my life and circumstances. Abba,
Father, I believe You are for me today. Amen.

Today's Reflection on Right Believing

....

....

....

DAY 60

How to Be "Undevourable"

Today's Scripture

Be sober, be vigilant; because your adversary the devil walks about like a roaring lion, seeking whom he may devour.
1 PETER 5:8

The devil doesn't want you to be strong in the Lord's love for you. Instead, he wants you to question God's love for you. To accomplish this, one of his key strategies is to try to make you think that God is mad at you.

God's Word tells us that the devil walks about like a roaring lion, *seeking* whom he may devour. This means that he cannot just devour anyone. He must look for those whom he *can* devour. Some of us are "*undevourable.*" There may not be such a word, but it certainly describes a great place to be when the enemy is on the prowl for his next victim.

My friend, you can become "undevourable" to the devil. The secret is found in the preceding verse, "casting all your care upon Him, for He cares for you" (1 Pet. 5:7). Can you see it? The secret to being "undevourable" is to be carefree and not be bogged down by anxieties and worries! It is to laugh a lot, enjoy your life, and to take no thought for tomorrow.

To the legalistic mind, this sounds terribly irresponsible. However, in God's mind, your greatest responsibility is to rejoice in the Lord always and to not worry about your past failures, your present circumstances, and your future challenges! Why? It's because of what God's grace has already done for you. And it's because the One who has the power over death is caring for you and watching over you right this minute.

If you want to see victory over the enemy's attacks, then learn to relax, to let go, and to release every oppressive thought, worry, and care into Jesus' loving hands. Believe with all your heart that He cares for you and that you are not alone in this journey. You have a constant companion in Jesus on this great adventure called life.

Note that the devil walks about *like* a roaring lion. The devil is an impostor who tries to intimidate you through the impression that God is angry with you. Let's be clear here: there is only one true lion and that is the Lion of Judah, Jesus Christ (see Rev. 5:5), the King of kings, and He is *not* mad at you today. His wrath is directed at anything that seeks to destroy you. You are not the object of His wrath; you are the object of His love. So be strong in His love for you. That's how you resist the devil who will have no choice but to flee from you!

Today's Thought
I can let go and release every negative thought, worry, and care into Jesus' loving hands. He is my constant companion on this great adventure called life.

Today's Prayer
Lord Jesus, You alone are the one true Lion of Judah, King of kings and Lord of lords. Thank You that I can be "undevourable" to the enemy as I cast every oppressive thought, worry, care, and fear into Your loving hands. I believe that You are my constant companion and that the enemy must flee because You are with me and for me. Amen.

Today's Reflection on Right Believing

DAY 61

Your Debt Has Been Paid

Today's Scripture

Therefore, brethren, having boldness to enter the Holiest by the blood of Jesus, by a new and living way which He consecrated for us, through the veil, that is, His flesh, and having a High Priest over the house of God, let us draw near with a true heart in full assurance of faith, having our hearts sprinkled from an evil conscience and our bodies washed with pure water.
HEBREWS 10:19–22

For decades upon decades, God has been portrayed as an angry God by the devil, and unfortunately, many Bible teachers have unwittingly helped him by painting a picture of a wrathful God. This depiction of God is an error. We are now under the new covenant, and you will not be able to find a single New Testament scripture that says God is angry with believers because of their sins. You would have to go into the Old Testament to look for verses that speak of God's anger at the sins of His people.

Does God not being angry with you mean that there is no place for God's correction in our lives? Is there correction and wise guidance that come by the Word of God in the new covenant of grace? Absolutely. But as for His anger toward you and your sins, all that has been settled at the cross. I guarantee you, when you come into Jesus' sweet presence with all your challenges, failings, and struggles, He is not going to roar at you. He is going to love you into wholeness and set you on a trajectory of freedom from all your fears, guilt, and addictions. Jesus is the end of all your struggles!

Because God's perfect love is the answer to overcoming the struggles in your life, the devil is doing everything he can to alienate and cut you off from this love. He knows that as long as the debt of sin is on your conscience, you will avoid God because you think that God is mad at you.

The beautiful thing about Jesus is that He not only paid the sin debt of your entire life, He *overpaid* it. Unlike the high priests of the Old Testament, He didn't offer the blood of bulls and goats to pay for your sins. This High

Priest paid for your sins with His own perfect and sinless blood. God didn't go soft on sin under grace! No way. He offered His only begotten Son, Jesus, who is an absolute overpayment for your sins.

It's as if you owed a debt of a million dollars, but Jesus paid a billion dollars to settle that debt. The truth is, if you knew who Jesus is and the value of the Son of God, you would know that His payment at the cross was worth more than a billion dollars. It's a payment that has wiped out your entire life's sins—past, present, and future—once and for all! No longer is there a chasm of sin separating you and God. It has been bridged by the bloodstained cross.

Today's Thought
Jesus is an overpayment for all my sins.

Today's Prayer
Father, thank You that because of who Jesus is, His sacrifice at the cross is a grand overpayment for my entire life's sins. I acknowledge that You did not go soft on sin, but that Jesus, my High Priest, paid for all my sins with His perfect, sinless blood. I believe that there is no longer any chasm separating me from You and that I can be bold to come before You to receive Your grace. Amen.

Today's Reflection on Right Believing

DAY 62

Sweet Intimacy with Jesus

Today's Scripture

*"...For as I have sworn that the waters of Noah would no
longer cover the earth, so have I sworn that I would not be angry
with you, nor rebuke you. For the mountains shall depart and
the hills be removed, but My kindness shall not depart from you,
nor shall My covenant of peace be removed,"*
says the LORD, *who has mercy on you.*
ISAIAH 54:9–10

Unfortunately, many sincere and well-meaning believers fall into the devil's trap, and they end up with the wrong belief that they have fallen short of God's expectations and have angered Him. They live in a constant state of trying to appease and please this angry God. Instead of enjoying a sweet, intimate relationship with Jesus, they feel like they are hypocrites or they feel as if they are always treading on eggshells when it comes to their walk with the Lord.

If you have experienced such thoughts about God before, I would like to share this very important principle with you: Fear and love cannot coexist in a healthy relationship. Insecurity and love cannot coexist in the truly intimate relationship that God wants with you and me, His children.

Let me share with you this letter I received from Lorraine who lives in Louisiana. I'll let it speak for itself as you soak in how you and your relationship with God can be completely changed by believing the right things about your heavenly Father. All I can say is, *Hallelujah!*

> *I have been a born-again Christian for twenty-two years. Today, at forty-four years old, I have a wonderful husband and beautiful daughter. I love my life!*
>
> *As far back as I can remember, I have always loved Jesus. But I had lived my entire life feeling guilty as I believed that God was always mad at me. I had always felt that I could not do enough "right" or "good" things. After I gave my life to Christ, that feeling of not being good*

enough actually got worse because I felt a greater responsibility to live up to a higher standard to be right with God. I was always repenting, always feeling that I'd done wrong and that my best was never enough.

I am in the process of reading Destined To Reign *and am only at chapter 9. I have to read this book very, very slowly so that I can digest its contents. I cannot tell you how my life has changed since I began reading your book. It was not until I began reading it that I felt relieved of the weight of not being good enough. It has shaken the very foundation of my world and dissolved the insecurity I've had about Jesus and His love for me.*

Forty-four years of my previously painful existence and mind-set are GONE. I am CHANGED forever. I am forgiven. I can't get through the rest of this book without stopping to thank the Lord for you and for giving you the message of grace to spread worldwide.

That's what it is all about, my friend. Winning the battle for your mind is all about your freedom and liberty in Christ Jesus, your Lord and Savior. When you start to believe right about His love and grace toward you, permanent, liberating change happens! So be strong in God's love for you and don't let wrong believing rob you of a life of great joy and peace. Remember, God is not mad at you; He is mad about you!

Today's Thought
God is not mad at me; He is mad about me.

Today's Prayer
Father, thank You that You have sworn that You would not be angry with me and that Your kindness would never depart from me. Thank You that through Jesus' sacrifice at Calvary, You have freed me from feeling that I have to be good enough or do enough right things to please You. I declare my liberty in Christ Jesus, and I believe that You are mad about me and that I live surrounded by Your love and favor today. Amen.

Today's Reflection on Right Believing

DAY 63

Not Self-Occupied but Christ-Occupied

Today's Scripture

I have been crucified with Christ; it is no longer I who live, but Christ lives in me; and the life which I now live in the flesh I live by faith in the Son of God, who loved me and gave Himself for me.

GALATIANS 2:20

As we press deeper into the power of right believing, I want to show you practical ways in which you can be transformed by the renewing of your mind. Right believing is all about renewing your mind and uprooting the wrong beliefs that shape your thinking and behavior. That's why the Word of God says, "Don't copy the behavior and customs of this world, but let God transform you into a new person by changing the way you think" (Rom. 12:2 NLT).

God wants to change the way we think by shifting our thoughts from self-occupation to Christ-occupation. Our human tendency is to be focused on ourselves. We are prone to excessive self-introspection and are easily susceptible to becoming preoccupied with ourselves rather than with Jesus. Many of our greatest pains, struggles, failures, and miseries stem from us being "I" centered. Oftentimes, we are engrossed with thoughts such as, "Have *I* done enough?", "What is wrong with *me*?" and "Why do *I* have so many weaknesses?" Unfortunately, when we become overly occupied with self, we become obsessed, oppressed, and inevitably depressed.

My friend, is your mind filled constantly with thoughts of how you have failed, how you have missed it, and how unworthy you are? That is symptomatic of someone who is clearly self-occupied. Thoughts like that cause a person to develop an inferiority complex. People who suffer from this are ever ready to condemn themselves. Their minds are clouded with negativity and pessimism.

But self-occupation can also manifest at the other end of the pendulum's swing as a superiority complex. There are people who think they are always better than everyone else. They are painfully arrogant, and they think their perspectives and opinions are always right. Whether you are feeling superior or inferior, your focus is still on yourself, and in the end that causes you great pain, misery, and heartache.

Only in Christ will you experience true transformation and walk neither in pride nor in false humility. When you are Christ-occupied, the flesh in you becomes inconsequential and you begin manifesting all the lovely, wholesome, and beautiful attributes of Jesus unconsciously. The fruit of the Spirit, such as love, joy, peace, and kindness, flow through you effortlessly when your mind is renewed and occupied with the person of Jesus. It's an inevitability! You cannot touch His grace and not become holy any more than you can touch water and not get wet.

_____

Today's Thought
Only in Christ will I experience true transformation and manifest His wholesome and beautiful attributes unconsciously.

Today's Prayer
Lord Jesus, thank You that when my mind is renewed and occupied with You, I experience true transformation and deliverance from an inferiority complex as well as pride. Thank You that as I fix my eyes upon You—as I just believe that You live in me, that my righteousness is of You, and that You are giving me the right motivations—true holiness will manifest as a result. I believe that Your life in me will cause the fruit of the Spirit to flow through my life effortlessly. Amen.

Today's Reflection on Right Believing

DAY 64

Supernatural Transformation

Today's Scripture

"You come to me with a sword, with a spear, and with a javelin. But I come to you in the name of the LORD of hosts, the God of the armies of Israel, whom you have defied."
1 SAMUEL 17:45

Christ-occupation makes you bold but not superior, humble but not inferior. When our minds are occupied with Jesus, we don't have to *try* to be humble. In the presence of the Servant-King, our hearts become supernaturally transformed, and we will carry His servant heart. In other words, when you hang out with Jesus, all that He is will rub off on you. Your thoughts and your words will be full of the fragrance of His sweet presence and grace. All your inferiority and insecurities will melt away in His marvelous love for you. It takes people who are truly secure in Christ to be able to bow down and serve others with genuine humility.

Similarly, when you are courageous and bold in Christ and in His love for you, it doesn't manifest as fleshly pride and arrogance, but rather as complete dependence on Almighty God. Think of how young David charged down the Valley of Elah and challenged the giant Goliath, while the rest of the well-trained and full-grown men of the army of Israel cowered in fear. Was that simply a display of youthful bravado or a genuine dependence on God?

To the untrained eye, David could have appeared like an impudent little brat. But we know where this steely chutzpah comes from when these bold words of a mere teenager resonated throughout the valley: "You come to me with a sword, with a spear, and with a javelin. But I come to you in the name of the LORD of hosts, the God of the armies of Israel, whom you have defied" (1 Sam. 17:45). From his words, we can tell that young David was clearly occupied with the Lord of hosts and not with himself or his abilities.

When your thoughts are occupied with the Lord, you become a giant slayer! Are there giants in your life today that need to be slain? Like young David, occupy your mind with the Lord, and God will fill you with the courage and audacity to overcome all your adversities. Listen to the words of David in Psalm 18:29: "For by You I can run against a troop, by my God I can leap over a wall." Let these words of faith and boldness be established in your heart. With God on your side, nothing is impossible!

Today's Thought

When my thoughts are occupied with the Lord,
I become a giant slayer!

Today's Prayer

Father, help me to keep my mind and heart focused on Jesus.
I want my thoughts and words to be filled with the fragrance
of His sweet presence and grace in my life. Like David, I declare
that by You I can run against a troop, and by You I can leap over a
wall. I believe that You are giving me the courage and audacity
to overcome all adversities in my life. With You on my side,
all things are possible! Amen.

Today's Reflection on Right Believing

DAY 65

Your Answer Is Found in a Person

Today's Scripture

O wretched man that I am! Who will deliver me from this body of death? I thank God—through Jesus Christ our Lord!

ROMANS 7:24–25

The flesh in us can produce a whole gamut of emotions and thoughts, from defeat, jealousy, greed, and lust to anger, inferiority, condemnation, and arrogance. As long as we are in this physical body, the flesh is active in us.

But we can rejoice because when Jesus died on the cross, the Word of God tells us that He "condemned sin in the flesh" (Rom. 8:3). All the negative thoughts and toxic emotions from the flesh have already been judged and punished at the cross. Today we can experience victory over the flesh through the power of the cross.

You can read all about the apostle Paul's struggle with the flesh in Romans 7:18–19: "For *I* know that in *me* (that is, in *my* flesh) nothing good dwells; for to will is present with *me*, but how to perform what is good *I* do not find. For the good that *I* will to do, *I* do not do; but the evil *I* will not to do, that *I* practice" (emphasis mine).

Did you notice how many times the words "I," "me," and "my" are mentioned in just the two verses above? I'm sure you can identify with the apostle Paul here in his struggle with the flesh. It's the struggle we all face when we are occupied with ourselves and warring with the flesh within us. It's a life of vexation, angst, defeat, and despair.

This is not where God wants you to live, my friend. A believer doesn't live in Romans chapter 7. Through Christ Jesus, we should be living in Romans chapter 8. Let's read on and discover how Paul broke free from this bondage of self.

Just a few verses later, Paul cries out, "O wretched man that I am! Who will deliver me from this body of death?" (Rom. 7:24). The answer, my friend, is found in a *person*, and Paul tells us this person is Jesus: "I thank God—through Jesus Christ our Lord!" (Rom. 7:25).

Only our beautiful Savior, Jesus Christ, can deliver us from the flesh. And in Christ we can step into the first verse of Romans chapter 8, which proclaims, "Therefore there is now no condemnation for those who are in Christ Jesus" (NASB). This is where we as new covenant believers ought to live. Not in the domain of constant struggle and despair, but in the domain of no condemnation and victory.

Today's Thought
Jesus is my answer to freedom from the bondage of self.

Today's Prayer
Father, thank You that through Jesus Christ You have delivered me from living in the flesh with all of its negative thoughts, toxic emotions, and struggles. I thank You that I can live freely in Romans 8 instead of Romans 7 today. I believe that there is no condemnation for me because I am in Christ Jesus. Amen.

Today's Reflection on Right Believing

DAY 66

The Lamb of God

Today's Scripture

"Behold! The Lamb of God who takes away the sin of the world!"
JOHN 1:29

I encourage you to start every new day with this thought: "God loves me and gave His only Son for me. Jesus is all for me today. I am saved, healed, favored, righteous, and accepted in Christ the Beloved."

Start your day by occupying your mind with Jesus. For a season in my life, before I even got out of bed, I would repeat to myself over and over again, "I am the righteousness of God in Christ." Some mornings I would say it more than fifty times. I wanted it to be a revelation pulsating in my heart, an unshakable belief that God is *for* me and *with* me. When you occupy your mind with Jesus, every struggle, fear, and bondage that you are entangled with will lose its evil grasp on you!

There is a beautiful picture of Jesus hidden in the Old Testament. Under the old covenant of the law, those who sinned were told to bring a sheep that was without blemish, wrinkle, or spot to the priest. The priest does not examine the person to see if he is perfect (without sin), because he has sinned. So the priest examines the sheep.

If the sheep is indeed perfect, the person who has sinned lays his hands on the sheep in an act of transferring his sins to the innocent sheep. At the same time, the innocence and perfection of the sheep are transferred to the person. The sheep is then killed, and the person leaves with his conscience cleared and his sin debt forgiven. He walks away under an open heaven of God's favor and blessing.

Can you see Jesus in this Old Testament practice? The sheep without blemish, spot, or wrinkle is a picture of the perfect Lamb of God, Jesus Christ Himself, who takes away the sins of the world. The priest is a picture of God. He doesn't examine you for your sins. Instead, He examines Jesus, and because Jesus is gloriously perfect, you can live today with your conscience cleared and your sin debt forgiven. You can walk under an open heaven and expect God's favor and blessings in your life. What a beautiful picture of God's abundant and lavish grace.

Today, turn your eyes away from yourself and stop the self-introspection! Look to Jesus, the Lamb of God, and see His perfection as your perfection. See His innocence as your innocence, His righteousness as your righteousness. Be occupied with Him, and be transformed from the inside out.

Today's Thought
Today, I choose to look to Jesus, the Lamb of God, and see His perfection as my perfection.

Today's Prayer
Lord Jesus, You are the perfect Lamb of God who has taken all of my sins away. I thank You that Your perfection has become my perfection and Your righteousness has become my righteousness. I believe that I walk under an open heaven of Your favor and blessings today. Amen.

Today's Reflection on Right Believing

DAY 67

Jesus, Be the Center

Today's Scripture

And He said to me, "My grace is sufficient for you, for My strength is made perfect in weakness." Therefore most gladly I will rather boast in my infirmities, that the power of Christ may rest upon me.

2 CORINTHIANS 12:9

I love how in Luke 24, the Holy Spirit intricately records for us the meeting that Jesus had with the two disciples on the road to Emmaus on the very first day of His resurrection. With heavy hearts, grieved and shell-shocked, they talked about how Jesus, whom they greatly esteemed, had been taken by the religious leaders, condemned to death, and crucified.

Read the full story and notice how the two disciples were caught up with their own understanding of the events that had transpired and with their thoughts about the redemption of Israel. As a result, they were downcast, disappointed, and depressed. This is what happens when the truth about Jesus is absent from our minds.

The disciples had hoped that Jesus would be the one who would redeem Israel. To them, Jesus was simply a means to an end. They were more consumed with Israel's redemption than with the Redeemer Himself. No wonder they were depressed! Jesus can never simply be a means to an end, no matter how noble that end may be. We need to be occupied with Him and allow everything to revolve around Him as He takes center place in our lives.

The disciples were downcast because they didn't believe in what God's Word had prophesied about Jesus' suffering and resurrection. If they had believed and understood that the events in the last three days were all orchestrated by God and that the cross was His grand redemption plan to save all men, they would have been rejoicing with faith, love, and hope. They would have been greatly anticipating their reunion with the resurrected Christ instead of being so inward-looking and discouraged. But because of their wrong beliefs, they had become disillusioned and were mentally defeated.

196

If you are feeling fearful, anxious, or depressed today, do a quick check. What's on your mind? What's your heart occupied with? Are your thoughts filled with faith in Jesus, the Shepherd of your life, or are they filled with apprehensions about the future, fears about your current situation, and excessive self-introspection? Give Him center place by believing that He is the answer to every thing you need in life, and begin to walk in a new measure of His peace, joy, and liberty.

Today's Thought

Today, I choose to rest in Jesus, the Shepherd of my life, instead of being fearful about my situation or my future.

Today's Prayer

Lord Jesus, I acknowledge that You can never simply be a means to an end in my life, even if it is a noble end. I want You to take the center place in my life. In every thing I do today, I choose to believe that You are the Shepherd of my life, and that Your grace is more than sufficient for me. I believe that as my heart is focused on You as Lord, You will deliver me from defeat to victory in all things. Amen.

Today's Reflection on Right Believing

DAY 68

Be Quick to Believe

Today's Scripture

Then He said to them, "O foolish ones, and slow of heart
to believe in all that the prophets have spoken!"
LUKE 24:25

In many places there are believers who still think that God is mad at them whenever they fail. They simply don't have a revelation of the gospel of grace and what God's unconditional love means. Like the two disciples on the road to Emmaus we read about yesterday, such believers still do not understand the grace of our Lord and what He has done for them at the cross.

Then there are believers who know about the gospel of grace and who even know that God loves them unconditionally. However, this knowing is only in their heads. When they fail, even though they have the knowledge of grace, they are nevertheless still afraid to come with boldness to God's throne of grace to receive mercy, favor, healing, and restoration.

Beloved, God doesn't want you slow of heart to believe His promise of abundant grace and gift of righteousness to reign in this life. Knowing God's truths and the gospel of grace intellectually is not enough. You have to be quick to believe everything that Jesus has accomplished on the cross for you, especially when you are struggling with failure, guilt, and fear. God doesn't want you defeated because of a lack of knowledge of His grace. At the same time, He wants you to be quick in believing in His promises for you.

This is why we study God's Word. It is not to merely accumulate Bible knowledge and historical facts, but to have a constant revelation of Jesus that feeds our quick and right believing in Him. And how do we do this? We can start by asking the Holy Spirit. Many times when studying the Word, I would pray this simple prayer: "Holy Spirit, open my eyes to see Jesus in the Word today." That is what it's all about—*seeing Jesus.* When you see Him in the Scriptures through the lens of grace, faith will arise and your mind will be renewed with His truths and promises for you.

My friend, you have already learned many things about God's love for you in this book. If you want to see the power of right believing operating in every dimension of your life, I challenge you to believe in His grace, His love, His righteousness, His forgiveness, and His finished work. I promise you that you will be transformed beyond your wildest imagination if you dare to lean hard on His love for you. His love never fails!

Today's Thought
*God wants me to see Jesus in the Word and to be quick
in believing in His promises for me.*

Today's Prayer
*Father, thank You for giving me Your Word to study. I ask You,
Holy Spirit, to open my eyes to see Jesus in the Word. I believe that
as You empower me to be quick to believe everything that Jesus
has accomplished on the cross for me, I will be transformed
beyond my wildest imagination. Amen.*

Today's Reflection on Right Believing

DAY 69

Ignite Your Heart

Today's Scripture

*"Did not our heart burn within us while He talked with us
on the road, and while He opened the Scriptures to us?"*
Luke 24:32

We've spent the last two days considering the experience of the two disciples on the road to Emmaus. What happened there that caused the disciples' hearts to ignite and burn within them? Go back to today's scripture and read it again. Therein lies the key to transformation! When the Scriptures are opened to you and things concerning Jesus are unveiled, your heart will be set aflame and burn within you as it did for these two disciples!

Don't forget what Jesus did when He heard their wrong believing and conversation of defeat: "Beginning at Moses and all the Prophets, He expounded to them in all the Scriptures *the things concerning Himself*" (Luke 24:27, emphasis mine). In other words, beginning with the first five books of Moses (Genesis, Exodus, Leviticus, Numbers, and Deuteronomy, collectively known as the Torah), Jesus expounded all the things concerning Himself. Then He continued to reveal Himself in the books of the prophets, books such as Samuel, Kings, Isaiah, and Jeremiah.

On the first day of His resurrection, Jesus set a precedent for us on how we ought to read and study the Bible today. He doesn't want us to approach the Word to find out what we need to do and go away with a bunch of laws. Absolutely not! Jesus wants us to open the Scriptures to see HIM. See Him in everything from Genesis to Revelation. The more you see Him, the more you will be free from all forms of self-occupation and be transformed from glory to glory.

I encourage you to open up the Bible and see Jesus in the types and shadows in the Old Testament. Every sacrifice, every feast, and even the tabernacle and priests point to Jesus. In the New Testament, see Jesus loving and forgiving those whom the world despised, such as the woman caught in adultery. See Him healing the blind, lame, and all who were oppressed with sicknesses and diseases. See Jesus multiplying provision for those who lacked. I promise you that your heart will burn, your body will be renewed, and your mind will be filled with His shalom-peace, joy, and soundness. I promise you that sin, addictions, bad habits, fear, guilt, anxiety, depression, and condemnation will drop off from your life when you are absorbed and occupied with the person of Jesus. They simply cannot coexist in your life when you are occupied with Christ and not yourself.

Today's Thought
Jesus wants me to open the Scriptures to see HIM—
His beauty, His grace, and His compassion.

Today's Prayer
Father, thank You that You invite me to read Your Word so
that I can see Jesus in the Scriptures from Genesis to Revelation.
I want my heart to be set aflame and burn as it did for the two
disciples on the road to Emmaus. I believe that the more I
see Jesus, the more I will be free from self-occupation and
transformed from glory to glory. Amen.

Today's Reflection on Right Believing

DAY 70

Open Up the Scriptures

Today's Scripture

So faith comes from hearing, and hearing
by the word of Christ.
ROMANS 10:17 NASB

When I was studying the Emmaus story, I asked the Lord why He chose to restrain the eyes of the two disciples such that they couldn't recognize Him. I asked Him, "Wouldn't it have been better for them to see You with Your nail-pierced hands?" Wouldn't it have been better if Jesus had walked down the busiest streets of Jerusalem, lifted up His hands, and hollered, "Yo! Everyone, check this out!"

But Jesus knew that doing that would not produce true faith. He revealed to me that it was more important for the disciples to see Him in the Word than to see Him in person. Wow, those words brought so much hope and encouragement to my heart. If the faith of the disciples was based on them seeing Jesus physically in the flesh, then what hope do we have today? Jesus purposefully restrained their eyes so that they would see Him first in the Scriptures. That places you and me on *equal ground* and with *equal opportunity* as the two disciples. Jesus wants us all to see Him in the Word.

God's Word tells us that "faith comes from hearing, and hearing by the word of Christ" (Rom. 10:17 NASB). This means that the more you hear Jesus unveiled, expounded upon, and pointed to in the Scriptures, the more faith will be imparted to your heart to believe everything God's Word says about you. Could it be that the reason many believers are still living in defeat today is that Jesus has not been unveiled in the Scriptures to them?

The gospel is all about Jesus. It's not about right doing. It's all about right believing about Jesus that makes a difference in people's lives. The apostle Paul says, "For I am not ashamed of the gospel of Christ, for it is the power of God to salvation for everyone who believes, for the Jew first and also for the Greek. For in it the righteousness of God is revealed from faith to faith; as it is written, 'The just shall live by faith'" (Rom. 1:16–17).

That's the gospel that I am not ashamed of. I pray that you will experience your own Emmaus Road journey as you open up the Scriptures and allow His Word to bathe your heart in the warmth of His loving grace and tender mercies. It's truly all about Jesus!

Today's Thought

I believe that as I see Jesus in the Word, faith, healing, strength, divine life, and the power of God will be imparted to me.

Today's Prayer

Father, thank You for the gospel of Christ. Thank You that all I have to do is believe the good news about Jesus, and that activates Your power to save me in every situation. I declare with the apostle Paul that I am not ashamed of the gospel of Christ, for it is Your power to save me. I believe that as I see more and more of Jesus unveiled in Your Word, more and more of Your loving grace and tender mercies will surround me. Amen.

Today's Reflection on Right Believing

DAY 71

Worship with the Words of David

Today's Scripture

But You, O Lord, are a shield for me, my glory and the One who lifts up my head. I cried to the Lord with my voice, and He heard me from His holy hill.

Psalm 3:3–4

When we are going through a difficult time or dealing with a heavy burden of stress, anxiety, fear, or condemnation, it's extremely challenging to make the paradigm shift from self-occupation to Christ-occupation. So how do we do it?

To answer that question, let me show you how David encouraged himself in the Lord whenever he was fearful, anxious, or depressed. Let's learn from someone whom God describes as "a man after My own heart" (Acts 13:22). God's Word reveals to us that whenever David was in trouble, he worshiped the Lord with beautiful psalms, hymns, and praises. Instead of wallowing in his own defeat and groping in darkness, David would turn his eyes to the heavens and lift up his voice to the King of kings.

In his closing years, when Absalom, his own son, betrayed him and tried to usurp the throne, David could have chosen to retaliate by sending out his loyal troops against Absalom. However, he didn't have the heart to fight against his beloved son. Instead David fled from Absalom with tears in his eyes and a broken heart. Just imagine how crushed David must have been.

But rather than be overwhelmed by the excruciatingly painful circumstances surrounding him, David looked to the Lord and worshiped Him with these eternal words as he ascended the Mount of Olives: "But You, O Lord, are a shield for me, my glory and the One who lifts up my head. I cried to the Lord with my voice, and He heard me from His holy hill" (Ps. 3:3–4).

Isn't it wonderful to know that when we cry out to God in worship, He hears us? As David worshiped the Lord, God turned his circumstances around for his good. God allowed a person in Absalom's camp to give him unsound advice, and as a result Absalom's coup d'état failed.

I am telling you that no matter what your trouble is today, learn to worship Jesus in your valley of trouble and praise His lovely name. See Him as your shield. See Him as your glory and the lifter of your head. Be consumed with Jesus, and He will turn your circumstances around for your good. Let your heart find rest and peace in the security of His love.

Today's Thought
Instead of being overwhelmed by my circumstances, I can cry out to God in worship knowing He hears me.

Today's Prayer
Lord Jesus, like David, I turn my eyes to the heavens and lift up my voice in worship to You, the King of kings. Thank You for hearing the cries of my heart from Your holy hill. I believe that You are my glory and the lifter of my head and that You will turn my circumstances around for my good. Amen.

Today's Reflection on Right Believing

DAY 72

The Power of Worship

Today's Scripture

Oh come, let us worship and bow down; let us kneel before the LORD our Maker. For He is our God, and we are the people of His pasture, and the sheep of His hand.

PSALM 95:6–7

Some people think that when they worship God, they are giving *something* to Him. On the contrary, I believe that as we worship and praise Him, *He is giving to us*, imparting His life, wisdom, and power into our lives, renewing our minds and physical bodies as well in His sweet presence.

Worship is simply a response on our part to His love for us. We don't have to, but when we experience His love and grace in our lives, we want to. It's a response birthed out of a revelation in our hearts of just how great, how awesome, how majestic, and how altogether lovely our Lord and Savior truly is. As we worship Him and become utterly lost in His magnificent love for us, something happens to us. We are forever changed and transformed in His presence. All fears, worries, and anxieties depart when Jesus is exalted in our worship.

We have seen this demonstrated through a worship collection, *A Touch of His Presence (Volumes 1 and 2)*, that we compiled from spontaneous worship songs that flowed from my spirit during intimate times of worship when we simply occupied ourselves with the person of Jesus. I would sing out what God was putting in my heart, and He would manifest His loving presence. That's when the gifts of the Spirit would operate and healings would break out among the people in the congregation.

We received a letter from Emma in Germany who said, "Whenever the devil tries to attack me with symptoms of a disease, I would listen to these worship CDs and worship Jesus, my Lord, my Savior, and my Redeemer. I would also often partake of the Holy Communion while listening to the worship songs. After a few minutes, all the symptoms would disappear!" Another brother described how this worship music freed him from paralyzing, irrational fear and chronic sleep problems.

I share these testimonies with you because I believe that some of you want to worship God, but you may not know where to begin when you are alone at home. If that sounds like you, then start by getting ahold of anointed Christian music that can fill your room with the presence of the Lord. Allow the music to simply wash over you like rivers of living waters. Let His presence flush out every fear and every anxiety. Let His love take away the cares that burden you. Let Jesus be magnified and glorified, and watch Him turn all things around for your good!

Today's Thought
All fears, worries, and anxieties depart when I come into Jesus' loving presence and exalt Him in worship.

Today's Prayer
Lord Jesus, thank You for showering me with Your love and grace. My only response is to worship and praise You for just how great, how awesome, how majestic, and how altogether lovely You are. I magnify and glorify You, Jesus, because You are altogether lovely and worthy of my whole life's worship. I believe that I am being changed in Your presence, that You are driving every fear and anxiety from me, and that You are turning every negative situation around for my good. Amen.

Today's Reflection on Right Believing

DAY 73

The Shepherd's Psalm

Today's Scripture

The LORD is my shepherd; I shall not want. He makes
me to lie down in green pastures; He leads me beside the
still waters. He restores my soul; He leads me in the paths of
righteousness for His name's sake…. Surely goodness and mercy
shall follow me all the days of my life; and I will dwell
in the house of the LORD forever.
PSALM 23:1–3, 6

Long before the enemy can steal your victory, he steals your song. Long before he can steal your joy, he steals your praise. Before you know it, you start becoming critical, pessimistic, moody, and depressed. Don't allow him to do that. Let praises be continually on your lips and always be conscious of the Lord's presence, His favor, His goodness, and His blessings in your life.

Don't know what to sing? There is no one better for us to learn from than the sweet psalmist of Israel, David. Aren't you glad that God gave us the book of Psalms in the Bible so we can worship the Lord with the words of David? God gave David a special gift to write songs that unveil His love and heart, so let's join David in exalting the name of the Lord and allow Him to become our rock and fortress when we feel besieged by the issues of life. Let's magnify the Lord and watch Him deliver us. Let's follow after Him and let Him be our Shepherd. Let Him bring us to rest in green pastures and lead us beside still waters.

Psalm 23 is an amazing psalm for you to memorize and meditate on every time you face a challenge. A brother in Maryland wrote me to share how he was healed of chronic pain in his shoulder simply by meditating on Psalm 23. John had read one of my daily devotionals on meditating on God's Word, where I demonstrated how to do this with Psalm 23. On his way home from work that very day, John began to meditate on "The Lord is my shepherd, I shall not want." He focused on how kind the Lord is to want to be our shepherd and how He has truly provided for all our needs. John saw the Lord protecting him on the road, healing him of his pain, and giving him favor at work. By the time he reached home, he discovered that the pain, which had plagued him for two years and restricted his movements, had completely left!

Something happens when you sing with the words of David. There is power to heal you right where you are. You will find your fears beginning to melt away. You cannot psych yourself out of fear. Maybe even as you are reading this right now, your mind is besieged with fear about your future or a fear of lack or of losing your youth. Perhaps you are afraid of some disease or of losing your loved ones to some sickness. Maybe you are tormented daily by the fear of rejection. My friend, the only fear God wants you to have is a wholesome fear of the Lord, which Jesus Himself defines as the *worship* of God. My friend, learn to worship the Lord and let His healing and peace permeate your mind, body, and external circumstances.

Today's Thought
*I choose to magnify the Lord today and allow
Him to be my Shepherd.*

Today's Prayer
Lord Jesus, I acknowledge that You are the good Shepherd who takes care of my every want, who makes me to lie down in green pastures, who leads me beside still waters and who restores my soul. Thank You for Your magnificent love for me. I exalt You, my rock and my fortress. I worship and magnify Your great name, and praise You, my healer and my provider. You alone are my deliverer and my protection from all harm and evil. Amen.

Today's Reflection on Right Believing

....

....

....

....

....

....

DAY 74

Choose to Bless the Lord

Today's Scripture

*I will bless the LORD at all times; His praise shall continually
be in my mouth. My soul shall make its boast in the LORD; the
humble shall hear of it and be glad. Oh, magnify the LORD
with me, and let us exalt His name together. I sought the LORD,
and He heard me, and delivered me from all my fears.*

PSALM 34:1–4

Psalm 34, one of David's most powerful psalms, was written by him in the cave of Adullam. I find it really interesting that David wrote it during one of the most challenging seasons in his life. It's by no stretch of the imagination for us to see that this was one of the lowest points in David's life—on the run from King Saul, full of fear and groveling in the presence of the king of Gath, then hiding in a cave. How the mighty had fallen!

After such a demeaning episode, in his darkest hour, David could have indulged in self-pity and condemnation, but instead he chose not to be defeated by his circumstances. Rather, he chose to bless the Lord and let the praises of the Lord be continually in his mouth. Was he fearful? Absolutely! However, despite his fear that King Saul would capture him or that the king of Gath would slay him to avenge Goliath, he sought the Lord in worship in that cave. And God in His faithfulness did not just deliver David from all his fears, but He also transformed all the men who were gathered in the cave with him. They went from being distressed, in debt and discontented to becoming fearless warriors, giant-slayers in their own right, and faithful, mighty men who served David all the days of their lives (see 2 Sam. 23:8–39).

Today, do you believe that God loves you and is faithful to deliver you? It doesn't matter if you are feeling fearful, if you are in distress, in debt, or discontented. Believe right. Believe that when you seek the Lord in worship as David did, the Lord will indeed hear you, deliver you from all your troubles and transform you. Worship is one of the easiest, yet most powerful ways of being free from self-occupation. Look away from the painful symptoms or the fearful circumstances that are bothering you, and worship Jesus. Be occupied with Him and everything will work together for your good.

Would you do me a favor? I would like you to visit josephprince.com/power, where I have included a worship video of me leading my church in singing the words of David in Psalm 34. I want to demonstrate to you through the video how worship is one of the quickest ways for you to focus on Jesus and overcome your feelings of defeat.

I am believing that as we worship the Lord, you will be completely free from any trouble or area of defeat that you are struggling with today. Let's agree together that your body will be healed, that all your fears will disappear, and that all your addictions will be gone in the mighty name of Jesus.

Come magnify the Lord with me, come worship Jesus with the words of David, and experience His goodness and deliverance!

Today's Thought

Worship is one of the easiest, yet most powerful ways of being free from self-occupation.

Today's Prayer

Father, I choose to bless Your name, and Your praise shall continually be in my mouth. I will magnify You and exalt Your great name. I believe that You hear me and that You are delivering me from all my fears. I believe that You will completely free me from any trouble or area of defeat. In the mighty name of Jesus, Amen.

Today's Reflection on Right Believing

DAY 75

Overcoming Fear

Today's Scripture

*And Jehoshaphat feared, and set himself to seek
the* L<small>ORD</small>, *and proclaimed a fast throughout all Judah.
So Judah gathered together to ask help from the* L<small>ORD</small>; *and
from all the cities of Judah they came to seek the* L<small>ORD</small>.

2 C<small>HRONICLES</small> 20:3–4

Have you been in a situation where your circumstances appear to be completely hopeless? Where you felt immobilized and overwhelmed by the challenges surrounding you, with no way out or even a temporary respite in sight? Perhaps under the accumulated weight of it all coming against you at once, you feel as if your entire life is spiraling out of control and falling apart.

That is exactly what happened to King Jehoshaphat and the small tribe of Judah when they were besieged on all fronts by three powerful and bloodthirsty armies rapidly advancing toward Jerusalem (see 2 Chron. 20). With their enemies mercilessly bent on annihilating them and all the inhabitants of Jerusalem, they were facing a forlorn and hopeless situation, and it looked as though they were bound for a tragic end.

When Jehoshaphat was informed that a great multitude was coming against him, his first reaction was fear! I don't know about you, but this gives me hope! I'm so glad that the Word of God gives us an authentic portrait of who Jehoshaphat was. He wasn't a valiant warrior king who was always full of faith and endowed with a disproportionate dose of fiery courage, always ready to take down his enemies. No, he was a regular guy. He did what you and I would have done—he panicked.

But what set Jehoshaphat apart was that even when he was fearful, the very first thing he did was to "set himself to seek the L<small>ORD</small>" (2 Chron. 20:3). That is something you and I need to learn to do as well whenever we are fearful. Instead of spiraling deeper into the abyss of self-defeat, know that when you are feeling overwhelmed by your circumstances, that is the time you need to set yourself to seek the Lord. It's certainly not the time to run away from

God or get bitter, angry, frustrated, and disappointed with Him. Hey, God is not the author of your troubles. He is the author and finisher of your faith, victory, and success.

Jehoshaphat shows us that it's quite all right to experience bouts of fear from time to time. God doesn't condemn you when you are afraid. But when you receive a negative medical report or some bad news about your family or business, set yourself to seek the Lord. Jesus is your answer! His perfect love for you will cast out all fear.

Today's Thought
*When I feel overwhelmed by my circumstances,
it is time to set myself to seek the Lord.*

Today's Prayer
*Lord Jesus, thank You that when I experience fear and feel
overwhelmed by all that life is throwing at me, the first thing
I can learn to do is to set my heart to seek You. You are the author
and finisher of my faith, my victory, and my success. I believe
that Your perfect love will cast out all my fears and lead
me to the victory I want to see. Amen.*

Today's Reflection on Right Believing

DAY 76

Having True Bible Hope

Today's Scripture

*"O LORD God of our fathers, are You not God in heaven,
and do You not rule over all the kingdoms of the nations,
and in Your hand is there not power and might, so that
no one is able to withstand You?"*

2 CHRONICLES 20:6

Yesterday, we saw that when faced with what appeared to be certain destruction, King Jehoshaphat set himself to seek the Lord. Today's scripture is part of his prayer.

Note that instead of rehashing his fears to the Lord and lamenting about how overpowered by their enemies their small tribe was, Jehoshaphat centered his prayer and thoughts on just how big and powerful his God truly is. He proclaimed boldly that "no one is able to withstand" the Lord—no one! In a hopeless situation, he *hoped* in the Lord.

I call that Bible hope! Hope is a beautiful word in the Bible. Hope in the New Testament is the Greek word *elpis*, which is defined as a "favorable and confident expectation" or "the happy anticipation of good."[4] This means that when you hope in the Lord, there is a joy in your countenance (simply put, a smile on your face). There is a confident assurance in your heart that, bleak as the circumstances appear to be, it's not over yet.

Unfortunately, the word "hope" as used in our modern vernacular is completely different and sometimes even antithetical to the way the Bible defines it. When we say things such as, "I hope that I will get the job," our use of the word connotes uncertainty, doubt, and ambivalence.

The Word of God declares that "this hope will not lead to disappointment. For we know how dearly God loves us" (Rom. 5:5 NLT). We can have true hope—a certain, joyful, confident expectation of good—when we rightly believe how dearly God loves us! There is a direct and proportionate correlation between hope and rightly believing in God's love for you. Hope springs in your heart when you believe that God loves you.

No matter how adverse your circumstances may seem today, put your trust in the Lord. Believe that God is working behind the scenes on your behalf, and that He is turning the situation around for your good (see Rom. 8:28). All His abundant heavenly resources, His power, His healing, His restoration, His deliverance, His provision, His favor, His help, His comfort, and His love are with you and on your side, waiting to be unleashed upon you. The Lord your God will open up the windows of heaven over your life and pour out for you such a blessing that there won't be room enough to receive it! When our entire hope and trust is in Him, we can count on His promises toward us. This hope never disappoints, which means that your greatest victories are ahead of you.

Today's Thought
I can have true hope—a certain, joyful, confident expectation of good—when I rightly believe how dearly God loves me!

Today's Prayer
Father, thank You that my hope in You can never lead to disappointment because it is rooted in how dearly You love me. As I face all that this day holds, I am joyful and confident that You will work in all of my situations to bring about good for me. I believe that my greatest victories lie ahead of me. Amen.

Today's Reflection on Right Believing

DAY 77

Stand Still

Today's Scripture

"Listen, all you of Judah and you inhabitants of Jerusalem, and you, King Jehoshaphat! Thus says the LORD to you: 'Do not be afraid nor dismayed because of this great multitude, for the battle is not yours, but God's.... You will not need to fight in this battle. Position yourselves, stand still and see the salvation of the LORD, who is with you, O Judah and Jerusalem!' Do not fear or be dismayed; tomorrow go out against them, for the LORD is with you."
2 CHRONICLES 20:15, 17

We have seen King Jehoshaphat set himself to seek the Lord and pray with hope before all the assembly of Judah. It was then that the Spirit of the Lord came upon Jahaziel, who spoke the words of the Lord that we read in today's scripture. On hearing these words of hope, all Judah humbled themselves before the Lord, bowing before Him and worshiping Him.

Today the Lord is saying the same words to you in your situation. Hope in Him for He loves you! You don't have to live in fear and discouragement when you know that the battle is not yours, but the Lord's. Stand still and see the salvation of the Lord. The battle is His, and you will not need to fight in it.

What do you do when you don't know what to do? The best thing you can do is to *stand still*. Stand still and see the salvation of the Lord in your situation.

But Pastor Prince, if I stand still, nothing will happen!

My friend, standing still is not inactivity or doing nothing. It's a posture of hope, and it involves keeping your hope anchored on the person of Jesus and having a sure and confident expectation of good. When the marauding armies of Pharaoh were charging toward the children of Israel, hell-bent on annihilating them, Moses simply declared to the terrified Israelites, "Do not be afraid. Stand still, and see the salvation of the LORD" (Exod. 14:13). The Hebrew word for salvation is *yeshua*, which is actually the name of Jesus. So salvation is the person of Jesus, and He is with you.

When you are caught in a hopeless situation, learn to position yourself—stand still and see the saving power of Jesus work on your behalf. He will never leave you nor forsake you (see Heb. 13:5). And as you center yourself, your thoughts, your beliefs, and your hopes on Him, He will lead you concerning what to do, just as He led Jehoshaphat to a triumphant victory over his enemies.

Today's Thought
When I stand still and put my trust in the Lord, I will see the saving power of Jesus work on my behalf.

Today's Prayer
Father, thank You that the battles I face in life are not my battles, but they are Yours. You will never leave me nor forsake me in any of life's situations. I believe that as I stand still and center my thoughts, my beliefs, and my hopes in You, You will show me Your salvation and lead me to victory. Amen.

Today's Reflection on Right Believing

DAY 78

Believe and Praise Him

Today's Scripture

"Hear me, O Judah and you inhabitants of Jerusalem: Believe in the
LORD your God, and you shall be established; believe His prophets,
and you shall prosper." And when he had consulted with the people,
he appointed those who should sing to the LORD, and who should
praise the beauty of holiness, as they went out before the army and
were saying: "Praise the LORD, for His mercy endures forever."
2 CHRONICLES 20:20–21

Today I want you to see two more powerful keys to winning life's battles from the account of King Jehoshaphat. The first is to believe in the Lord, and you will be established. God's Word tells us also to believe the words of His prophets (the pastors and preachers whom God has placed in your life), and you shall prosper! That is the power of right believing. Don't be myopic and be caught up with your current challenges, running around like a headless chicken, trying to solve your problems in your own strength. God doesn't want you to live in a perpetual state of uncertainty, anxiety, stress, and fear. When you believe right, you will experience true Bible hope and start living with a certain, joyful, confident expectation of good regardless of your current circumstances.

The second key is to go into battle singing praises to God. This was what Jehoshaphat did. It may have been an unusual military strategy, but as the Israelites began to sing and praise, God caused confusion among the enemies' camps, and they utterly destroyed one another. Judah did not draw a single sword that day, but the battle was won. In fact, it was won before Judah's troops even arrived at the scene.

God deliberately records for us the words with which the people of Judah praised Him: "Praise the LORD, for His mercy endures forever." Psalm 118 begins and ends with this same refrain—a refrain so close to God's heart that it features very prominently in many key moments in Israel's history (see 1 Chron. 16:7, 34; 2 Chron. 7:3). My friend, there is something very special

229

about these two simple lines of praise. The word for "mercy" here is the very potent Hebrew word *hesed*, which speaks of God's grace, love, tender mercies, and loving-kindness.[5] No matter how many times you have failed and fallen short, and even if the troubles that surround you are a consequence of your own actions, would you turn to the Lord today and praise Him for His goodness and His *hesed* (His grace)?

When you are feeling down, overwhelmed, or fearful, worship Him with these words, and as you praise Him, He will "set ambushes" against all your enemies, troubles, fears, challenges, and addictions, as He did for Jehoshaphat and the people of Judah (see 2 Chron. 20:22). By the time you reach your battlefield, I believe your enemies will all have fallen. Not a single one of your adversaries will escape because the Lord Himself fights your battles.

Today's Thought

I will praise the Lord, for His mercy endures forever.

Today's Prayer

Lord Jesus, I praise You for who You are and for Your grace, love, tender mercies, and loving-kindness that endures forever. I believe that because You love me, You fight my battles for me. I declare that as I believe in You, I shall be established, and as I believe the words of Your prophets, I shall prosper. Because You fight my battles, I shall triumph over all of my enemies, fears, challenges, and addictions. Amen.

Today's Reflection on Right Believing

DAY 79

Ask Big

Today's Scripture
*"And whatever you ask in My name, that I will do,
that the Father may be glorified in the Son."*
JOHN 14:13

I want to begin this day by giving you this challenge: ask God for big things! What do you desire to see in your life—in your family, health, finances, and career? What would you ask God for if you knew beyond the shadow of a doubt that He is good and that His love for you endures forever? Ask God for them! Jesus came so that you might live a life that is marked not by lack, but by abundance; not by despair, but by the fullness of His love, joy, and peace.

I would like you to write down in your journal what you would ask God for if you knew that He hears your prayers. What are your dreams, hopes, and aspirations? What would you like to see come to pass in your life? What are you battling with today? Which area of your life would you like to see God's power work in? Write it down. Write it all down. Write what you want to see happen with Bible hope in your heart that He hears you and will supply. Write with a certain, joyful, positive, and confident expectation of good.

Don't just ask God for small things. Ask Him for big things! For instance, don't ask Him for just a job. Ask Him for a position of influence. Don't just ask Him to restore your health. Ask Him for a long and healthy life filled with many good days. Enlarge your faith to believe in God's goodness. He is pleased when our faith is big. He is not offended when we ask Him for big things.

Would you do that right now? Just take a few moments and pen down your requests to God—God, who is almighty and more powerful than we can ever imagine. God, who hung the planets in their places and spoke order into the world. God, who led His people in a pillar of cloud by day and a pillar of fire by night. God, who rained manna from heaven and brought forth water from dry rock. God, who turned bland waters into the finest wine. God, who made the lame walk, the blind see, and the deaf hear. God, who multiplied five loaves of bread and two small fish to feed five thousand men. God, who raised the dead and conquered the grave.

Ask what you need of God, who loves YOU with an everlasting love!

Today's Thought
God is pleased when my faith is big and I ask Him for big things.

Today's Prayer
Father, thank You for Your great love that invites me to boldly ask You for whatever I need. Thank You that You care about my dreams, hopes, and aspirations, and that I can come before You confidently and ask for big things. I believe that You hear my prayers and will answer because of Your everlasting love for me. Amen.

Today's Reflection on Right Believing

DAY 80

God Loves It When You Ask of Him

Today's Scripture

*"Ask, and it will be given to you; seek, and you will find;
knock, and it will be opened to you. For everyone who asks receives,
and he who seeks finds, and to him who knocks it will be opened.
Or what man is there among you who, if his son asks for bread,
will give him a stone? Or if he asks for a fish, will he give him a
serpent? If you then, being evil, know how to give good gifts
to your children, how much more will your Father who is
in heaven give good things to those who ask Him!"*
MATTHEW 7:7–11

There was a man in the Bible by the name of Jabez. His name was rather unfortunate. It means "sorrow"[6] because his mother "bore him in pain" (1 Chron. 4:9). What a name to have! But Jabez cried out to God, "Oh, that You would bless me indeed, and enlarge my territory, that Your hand would be with me, and that You would keep me from evil, that I may not cause pain!" (1 Chron. 4:10).

Some preachers claim that believers should not pray "selfish" prayers for themselves to be blessed. Jabez' prayer would probably fall under their definition of a "selfish prayer" as it was all about him asking God to bless him, enlarge his territory, be with him, and protect him. But God didn't reprimand Jabez for asking Him for these blessings. Without any fanfare, the Bible in the very same verse simply records that "God granted him what he requested."

That was all. No drama, no long list of what Jabez had to do or not do. It's really that simple. God heard his prayer and granted his request! No rebuke, no instructions, no "Jabez, if you want Me to bless you, you must first do this." No, God honored the man's faith and turned his sorrow into *joy* and his pain into *blessings*—all because he had an unshakable confidence in how good God is and asked big!

My friend, have a good opinion of God. He is not out to get you. He loves you and desires to unleash His favor into every area of your life. He loves it when you call upon Him. And He promised that He would answer when you do. Just see Him declaring to you Jeremiah 33:3: "Call to Me, and I will answer you, and show you great and mighty things, which you do not know."

Could it be that we are not seeing many breakthroughs because we have made asking God for big things a taboo with our religious and legalistic rhetoric? Could it be that we are just not seeing many blessings because we have not been asking God and seeking Him with a confident expectation of good?

My friend, it gives your heavenly Father great joy when you ask Him. It's His good pleasure to bless you as well as your family (see Luke 12:32). Stop being held back by erroneous beliefs about God, and start asking Him for whatever is on your heart today!

Today's Thought

It gives my heavenly Father great joy when I call upon Him.
He has promised that He will answer when I do.

Today's Prayer

Father, thank You that just as Jabez did, I can ask You to
bless me, to enlarge the territory of my life, to be with me, and to
protect me. I believe that You love me and desire to unleash Your
favor into every area of my life. Answer the cries of my heart
and show me great and mighty things that You have in store
for me because You love me. Amen.

Today's Reflection on Right Believing

DAY 81

God Honors Our Faith

Today's Scripture

Then Joshua spoke to the LORD in the day when the LORD delivered up the Amorites before the children of Israel, and he said in the sight of Israel: "Sun, stand still over Gibeon; and Moon, in the Valley of Aijalon." So the sun stood still, and the moon stopped, till the people had revenge upon their enemies...for the LORD fought for Israel.
JOSHUA 10:12–14

Joshua, Moses' successor who led the children of Israel into the promised land, was someone who dared to ask big. When Joshua was caught in the thick of battle with his enemies and the sun was about to set, he cried out for the sun and moon to stand still, and the Bible goes on to record that God answered his prayer.

I love this story. When my leaders and I were in the plains where this battle took place, we could see the sun over Gibeon on one side and the moon over the Valley of Aijalon on the other side. Both the sun and moon could be seen at the same time from that location. Standing there, I could just imagine Joshua in the midst of the battle, raising his voice and pointing to the sun on one side to stand still and then turning to the moon to issue the same command. Joshua was asking God for more daylight because the momentum of the battle was to their advantage. He wanted to completely rout his enemies and not give them time to regroup.

When you think about what Joshua asked, it was both an audacious and inaccurate request! If you were attentive during your science classes in school, you know that the earth orbits around the sun, not the sun around the earth! So technically, when Joshua called for the sun and moon to stand still, God made the *earth* stand still instead. Joshua's request was scientifically inaccurate, but nevertheless, God honored Joshua's chutzpah faith! He understood that what Joshua needed was more daylight, and He made it happen.

Isn't it encouraging to know that God didn't correct Joshua and give him CliffsNotes on how the solar system that He built actually functions? It gives me great encouragement to know that even when our faith confessions may not always be perfect, God still honors our hope and faith in Him. He loves it when we ask Him for big things. My friend, you can ask of Him, knowing that the battle truly belongs to the Lord, and that He will fight for you the way He fought for Israel because you are His covenant child.

Today's Thought
I can boldly ask God for the breakthroughs I want to see, knowing that my battles truly belong to Him, and that He fights them for me.

Today's Prayer
Father, thank You that You don't demand perfection when I ask You for big things. You know my heart and honor my hope and faith in You. I believe that today's battle truly belongs to You, and that You will fight for me the way You fought for Israel because I am Your covenant child. Amen.

Today's Reflection on Right Believing

DAY 82

Nothing Is Impossible

Today's Scripture

Now to Him who is able to do exceedingly abundantly
above all that we ask or think, according to the power that
works in us, to Him be glory in the church by Christ Jesus
to all generations, forever and ever. Amen.
EPHESIANS 3:20–21

Abandoned at birth and adopted by an illiterate widow, she was raised together with four other orphans in a little village in Perak, Malaysia. Life was hard in their tiny makeshift hut with a leaky zinc roof and no running water or electricity. At only nine years of age, she started working in a dusty factory after school, pulling rigid strips of rattan to weave them into bags for a little less than an American nickel per bag, so that her family had food. It seemed her life was destined to be trapped in a cycle of poverty.

Despite her challenging circumstances, this lady shared with me that even as a child, she had always felt there was a God somewhere, who was watching over her, protecting her, and blessing her. She remembered praying a simple, innocent prayer to this unknown God, saying, "If You are the true God, please come and look for me so that I may come to know You." She had no idea that her Father in heaven had an amazing plan for her life.

She did so well in school that her vice principal encouraged her to continue her studies in Singapore. With her adopted mother's blessing and only ten Malaysian dollars in her pocket, she headed to Singapore. Despite having to take on various jobs to support herself as well as her family, she continued to thrive in her academic pursuits, went on to a top-tier local university, and graduated with honors in chemistry. She then landed a well-paying job at a multinational company. After three and a half years, she decided to venture out to build her own business in 1989.

In the year 2000, God honored the prayer that she had prayed as a young child when a friend invited her to New Creation Church in Singapore. Having heard different things about God over the years, she remembers the freedom that she experienced when she learned for the first time through my preaching on grace that God loved her so much more than she could ever love Him. She stopped seeing God as someone far away and instead had a personal encounter with Jesus.

Some time later, she felt the Lord leading her to take her business public to remain competitive. She presented her business plan to a bank for its assistance to underwrite her company's attempt to undertake an initial public offering (IPO). The bank manager declined, explaining that it was not the right time to attempt an IPO as the Dow Jones had been on a massive downward slide. Half-jokingly he said, "If the Dow Jones starts going up today, come back tomorrow and we can talk again."

When she walked out of the bank, she remembered a message that I had preached on being bold and asking God for big things. She said, "You told us not to insult God by asking only for small things. You said, 'Ask God for big things, compliment Him and have a positive, confident expectation of good.'" So before going to bed, she asked God to do a big thing for her. She simply prayed and believed, "God, You are Almighty. Surely You can influence the US market and make the Dow Jones go up in Jesus' name." Now, Singapore is twelve hours ahead of New York, so the market opens when it is night in Singapore. At about 4 a.m., this lady felt a prompting to get out of bed to check on how the Dow Jones was doing…and found that it was beginning to climb upward! In the space of just four hours, the Dow Jones had risen by an astonishing 18 percent.

Pastor Prince, can God do things like this?

Of course He can. Anything is possible for those who believe God and have a confident expectation of good. This lady had the boldness to ask God to bless her and turn things around for her, just as Jabez did, and God answered her request.

With God's favor, her IPO was underwritten and her company went public. Remarkably, at that very time the Singapore government launched an initiative to highlight the importance of recycling wastewater into drinkable water and released news of a big tender to build the nation's first wastewater recycling and treatment facility. She knew absolutely nothing about this project and was just keeping her eyes on Jesus. Nobody could have orchestrated the media hype, publicity, and excitement over water—her very industry. Her company's IPO became a sensational hit and was oversubscribed seven times. Her company, Hyflux, became the first water treatment company to be listed on the Singapore Exchange.

She shared with me so many other amazing testimonies of how the Lord continued to open doors of favor and blessings for her in China, India, and the Middle East after the public listing of her company. When she submitted tenders for multimillion-dollar infrastructural projects to build wastewater plants or some of the largest membrane-based seawater distillation facilities in the world, she would be the little David among the Goliaths in the industry. Yet she came up tops, and many times was awarded the projects. That, my friend, is called the *favor* of God.

In 2011, Olivia Lum, in a competitive field with close to fifty top-notch entrepreneurs from around the world, was accorded the prestigious Ernst & Young World Entrepreneur of the Year award, the first woman to be recognized with this honor. In her acceptance speech, she thanked her Lord Jesus Christ.

How does a young girl who was abandoned at birth go from weaving rattan bags for a nickel to building a billion-dollar, public-listed company? That is the power of right believing, my friend. Nothing is impossible when you believe right in the person of Jesus and in His love and goodness. It's not how or what you begin with. You may have been born under severely challenging circumstances, or perhaps your parents are separated, or you may even have suffered abuse as you were growing up. My friend, I am here to tell you that with God in your life, it's *not* the end of the road! You can have hope and expect good even when things in your life seem hopeless. See His love for you. Believe that He has amazing plans for your life, and ask God for big things.

Today's Thought

Nothing is impossible when you believe right in the person of Jesus and in His love and goodness.

Today's Prayer

Father, absolutely nothing is impossible with You. It's not about where I was born or what challenges I've faced or am facing now. I believe that with You in my life, I can expect good even when life seems hopeless, and I can walk in all the amazing plans You have for me. Amen.

Today's Reflection on Right Believing

DAY 83

What Are You Hearing about Jesus?

Today's Scripture

She had heard about Jesus, so she came up behind him through the crowd and touched his robe. For she thought to herself, "If I can just touch his robe, I will be healed." Immediately the bleeding stopped, and she could feel in her body that she had been healed of her terrible condition.

MARK 5:27–29 NLT

Perhaps like the woman with the issue of blood in the Gospels (see Mark 5:25–34), you are facing an impossibly hopeless situation in your life. It could be a debilitating sickness, a marital situation, a financial crisis, or a prolonged challenge. In the natural, the future looks dismal and there appears to be no reason to hope. If that is you, I encourage you to believe that you too can experience the kind of breakthrough this woman experienced.

Imagine: for twelve long years, she had watched helplessly as her condition went from bad to worse no matter what she tried. Most of us would have given up. How did she find hope in the midst of her hopelessness? What gave her the courage to hope again?

I believe that the secret to her faith can be found in these five words: "She had heard about Jesus."

What do you think she heard about Jesus? This is an important question because whatever she had heard imparted an audacious sense of Bible hope and confidence in her. And this imbued her with a boldness and tenacity to risk everything just to touch the hem of His garment. She knew well the religious laws concerning unclean persons such as herself meant that she could be subjected to public humiliation and, very possibly, violence if she was recognized. Clearly she must have had no doubt in her heart that she would be completely healed the moment she touched the hem of His garment or she would not have risked it.

The Bible does not tell us exactly *what* she heard about Jesus, but I submit to you that she must have heard story after story of how Jesus healed the sick everywhere He went, how good and gracious He was even to the unclean lepers or the down-and-out who came to Him. What she heard about Jesus produced in her a positive, confident expectation of good, which we can see in what she declared: "If only I may touch His clothes, I shall be made well." This hope then resulted in a faith that was effortless.

Faith as defined in God's Word is "the confidence that what we hope for will actually happen" (Heb. 11:1 NLT). In other words, the hope that she had in the goodness of Jesus became faith, and this faith gave her the boldness to press through the crowd and receive her healing from Jesus.

What are you hearing about Jesus? The more you hear about His goodness and grace, the more faith will unconsciously arise in you to receive your miracle.

Today's Thought

*Faith becomes effortless when I keep hearing and hearing
about Jesus' goodness and grace.*

Today's Prayer

*Lord Jesus, You free the captives and heal all who come to You.
You love the despised, the unclean, the disdained, the scorned,
the rejects of society, and You transform their lives with Your grace.
What a loving and compassionate Savior You are! Thank You
that I am hearing the truth about You. I believe I can touch
You by faith right now and be made whole. Amen.*

Today's Reflection on Right Believing

....

....

....

....

....

DAY 84

Hearing Right Produces Right Believing

Today's Scripture

My child, pay attention to what I say. Listen carefully to my words. Don't lose sight of them. Let them penetrate deep into your heart, for they bring life to those who find them, and healing to their whole body.

Proverbs 4:20–22 NLT

Hearing plays a huge part in right believing. You cannot believe right unless you are hearing right. Man, that was good! I don't want you to miss that. *You cannot believe right unless you are hearing right.* I believe the woman in yesterday's reading began to believe right when she began to hear right. God's Word tells us that "faith comes from hearing, that is, hearing the Good News about Christ" (Rom. 10:17 NLT).

What you hear is vital. If you are believing God for a breakthrough in your life, pay attention to what you are listening to. Are you hearing messages that are full of the good news of Jesus? After you listen to these messages (or read these resources), are you filled with the heavy sense of what *you need to do*? Or are you filled with the empowering sense of who Jesus is in your life and everything *He has done for you* at the cross?

According to the law, the woman with the issue of blood was unclean, unworthy, and disqualified. If she had heard that Jesus was no different from the religious Pharisees of her day, there was no way she would have had a positive expectation of good. Under the law, when the unclean touches the clean, the clean becomes unclean. But under the grace of God, when the unclean touches the clean (Jesus), the unclean becomes clean! This woman didn't defile Jesus with her uncleanness when she reached out and touched His garments. On the contrary, she was infected with Jesus' health and wholeness and made completely whole. Oh, the beauty and the depths of God's amazing grace!

What have you been hearing about Jesus? Are you hearing about a hard, legalistic, and religious Jesus who is demanding, harsh, and unforgiving? Or are you hearing the true good news of His love, grace, and tender mercies toward you?

The true gospel of grace always imparts hope and faith to you to believe in Jesus and His goodness. No matter how long you have been struggling or how long it has been since you saw any results, I want to encourage you to fill your ears, eyes, and mind with the good news of Jesus. Trust me, when you incline your ear to messages that are all about His grace, you will inevitably begin to have a positive, confident expectation of good. When your heart is filled with hope through hearing all the amazing stories about Jesus, like the woman, you'll reach out in faith. Beloved, reach out and receive your miracle and freedom from your loving Savior today!

Today's Thought
I cannot believe right unless I am hearing right.

Today's Prayer
Father, the beauty and the depths of Your grace as expressed in the good news of Jesus are amazing! Thank You for revealing the beauty, grace, and goodness of Jesus to me through Your Word today. I ask You to keep showing me everything Jesus has done for me at the cross. As I keep hearing about His grace, I believe I will receive my miracle and freedom from every bondage. Amen.

Today's Reflection on Right Believing

....

....

....

....

....

....

....

DAY 85

The Power of Hearing Right

Today's Scripture

Therefore He who supplies the Spirit to you and works miracles among you, does He do it by the works of the law, or by the hearing of faith?

GALATIANS 3:5

Not too long ago, I received an email from George, who lives in California. He shared that he had been diagnosed with Evans syndrome, a rare autoimmune disease where a person's antibodies attack his or her own red blood cells and platelets. At one point, this brother had to be rushed to the emergency room because he was at risk of spontaneous bleeding. His blood platelet count had dropped dramatically to just 4,000/mcL (the normal range for a healthy person is between 150,000 and 400,000/mcL).[7] This is what George wrote:

The doctors administered infusions of blood products and had me on super-high doses of steroids. The steroids, which I reacted terribly to, made me so depressed and at one point suicidal. I couldn't think or even have normal conversations. I cried constantly. Our three kids didn't know what to think of what was happening to their daddy. I actually started telling people that God was punishing me for things I had done.

Every time I received an infusion and the doctors upped my steroid dosage, my platelets went up to a normal range, but it would never last for very long. My immune system continued attacking and destroying my platelets no matter what treatment I was getting. I was constantly getting my blood drawn, constantly checking to see what my count was, constantly aware of all the symptoms Evans was causing and the side effects of my medication.

Then, somewhere in the middle of all of this, the Holy Spirit led me to your television ministry. By the grace of God, I ended up on a channel I had never turned to before and saw the Grace Capsule. The lady on the phone told me that it would take one to three weeks for it to arrive, but it came in two days!

251

And let me tell you, your Grace Capsule was a gift from God. Through your teachings, Daddy God showed me His love. I went from feeling condemned, feeling like God was punishing me, to beholding the finished work of Jesus on the cross. He miraculously took all the bondages in my life away—the cigarettes, the pornography, the marijuana, everything that had been a struggle.

I had had back pain and acid reflux for years, but by listening over and over again to your sermons and hearing them constantly—at home or in the hospital, all through the night—the pain and acid reflux went away. It is now four months later, and PRAISE BE TO JESUS, I still have no acid reflux or back pain!

Three months ago, my spleen was removed with the hope that the Evans syndrome would go away, or at least be lessened. But even after the surgery, my count dropped again. The only two options for treatment were more severe in our minds—one of them being chemotherapy. By this time, I'd been listening to the Grace Capsule for about a month, and finally I decided to give the Evans syndrome to God. I stopped doing blood counts, stopped giving weight to all of my symptoms, and started thanking the Lord for my complete healing.

Now Jesus has restored everything to me better than it was before. He has given me more strength, more energy, and a lot more love. I thought I understood love before, but now I know what true love is because of my Father's love and Jesus' love for me. I haven't had a count done in months. My wife and I take the Lord's Supper every day. We thank Jesus every day for healing us with the stripes He bore for us. All praises be to Him!

You may be wondering what the Grace Capsule is. It's an MP3 player preloaded with more than seventy hours of messages that I had personally selected from my message library. Each message is full of the person of Jesus and His grace.

Beloved, I want to encourage you to listen and keep listening to messages that are all about Jesus as this brother did. You can't worry your problems away, but I believe that you can certainly listen your problems away. Faith indeed comes by hearing and hearing the good news of Christ!

Today's Thought
Listen and keep listening to messages that are all about the good news of Christ.

Today's Prayer

Father, thank You that there is power in reading and hearing messages that are all about Jesus and His grace. Help me to make listening to anointed messages of Jesus a daily priority. I acknowledge that I cannot worry my problems away, but I believe that by hearing the good news of Jesus, faith to receive every miracle I need will come. Amen.

Today's Reflection on Right Believing

DAY 86

Satisfied by Grace Every Day

Today's Scripture

And Jesus said to them, "I am the bread of life. He who comes to Me shall never hunger, and he who believes in Me shall never thirst."
JOHN 6:35

I want to encourage you to make listening to the good news of Jesus a daily priority. Listen, I know just how crazy and busy our days can get. But when the day is over and we have heard nothing about Jesus, we feel empty, stressed out, worried, fearful, and depressed.

My friend, Jesus is the bread of life and the living water. No matter how busy we get, it is prudent not to neglect feeding on His person. I know that in the natural, this can sound simplistic. You may be asking yourself, "How can simply listening about Jesus change things in my life and circumstances?" The truth is, the things of God are really not complicated. Just think about the woman who suffered from hemorrhaging for twelve years. Simply hearing about Jesus and His grace infused her with so much hope, so much faith, and so much courage that she was able to receive the healing she had started to believe for. Don't underestimate the power of hearing about Jesus just because it sounds simple.

There is a beautiful verse in the psalms that says, "Teach us to number our days, that we may gain a heart of wisdom" (Ps. 90:12). Do you want to know the secret of numbering your days and not allowing a single day of your life to be put to waste? The key is found in verse 14, where it says, "Oh, satisfy us early with Your mercy." The word "mercy" here is the Hebrew word *hesed*, which means God's grace.[8] God is telling us to be satisfied every day with His grace.

I suggest that before you do anything—read the papers, check your emails, or make that important phone call—start the day with Jesus and be satisfied with His grace. You can read a devotional about God's grace, feed on the Father's love, meditate on His grace, listen to a message that is all about Jesus, and open up His love letter—His Word—to you.

254

But Pastor Prince, my mornings are crazy! How long do I spend doing this? How much must I read, listen, or pray?

Beloved, the key is not to be legalistic about it. If morning doesn't work for you, then find a time that best suits your schedule. It could be during your lunch break or just before you go to bed. The key principle here is to be *satisfied* daily with His grace. Feed on Him until your heart is full and satisfied with His grace. It's really not about the duration or how much, but your level of satisfaction.

Enjoy God's presence daily. He loves having a relationship with you and wants to fill your heart with His grace, peace, wisdom, and joy.

Today's Thought
Feeding on my Father's love and meditating on His grace are key to gaining a heart of wisdom and living a life of wholeness.

Today's Prayer
Lord Jesus, thank You that You are the bread of life and the living water that satisfies the depths of my soul with grace. Thank You for inviting me to feed upon Your love and to meditate on Your grace. I believe that as I listen to Your good news You will satisfy me with Your tender mercies and give me a heart of wisdom so that not a single day of my life will be put to waste. Amen.

Today's Reflection on Right Believing

DAY 87

Unveiling the Heart of the Father

Today's Scripture

*"And he arose and came to his father. But when he was still
a great way off, his father saw him and had compassion, and ran and
fell on his neck and kissed him…. But the father said to his servants,
'Bring out the best robe and put it on him, and put a ring on his
hand and sandals on his feet. And bring the fatted calf here and
kill it, and let us eat and be merry; for this my son was dead
and is alive again; he was lost and is found.'"*
LUKE 15:20, 22–24

One of the most beautiful parables in the Bible is the parable of the father of the prodigal son (Luke 15:11–32). Many commentators call this the parable of the prodigal son, but the real hero of this story is the father and his love for his two sons. It's a parable that Jesus used to skillfully unveil to us the true heart of our gracious and loving heavenly Father.

Please take a few minutes to read through the full parable, and as you read through it, consider this: What is your opinion of God, especially when you've made a mistake? Do you see Him as an all-powerful, distant, and unfeeling judge who is angry whenever you fail and who constantly has to be appeased? Or do you know Him as your Daddy, your Abba Father whom you can run to anytime, even when you have fallen short? Do you see Him as unwaveringly and patiently waiting for you to return to Him and then racing down the road to meet you with tears streaming down His face, embracing you, and raining His kisses upon you?

As I was studying the Word, the Lord revealed to me that many believers have come to a place where they have forgotten their heavenly Father. They have forgotten about His love, His grace, and His loving-kindness. They relate to God in a judicial and transactional fashion, coming before Him with apprehension and trepidation, presenting their failings to Him and quickly leaving before they get the punishment and condemnation *they think* they rightly deserve from Him. They perceive Him *exclusively* as a God of holiness, judgment, and justice—His face steely and stern, His mighty arms folded in dissatisfaction and disapproval. They see a God who is easily displeased, quick to anger, perpetually disappointed with them, and waiting impatiently to be placated.

This wrong belief of who God really is has driven many into fear, guilt, depression, and insecurity. And that is why it's so vital we see the heart of the Father as unveiled by Jesus in this timeless parable.

Beloved, do you see His heart of love for you? There is a vacuum in our hearts that can only be filled by the Father's love. I believe that if you would allow the Father to come into your heart today and fill you up with His perfect love, you will find the joy, confidence, fulfillment, and freedom that you have been looking for in life.

Today's Thought
*Only the Father's perfect love can fill the vacuum in my heart
and bring the joy, confidence, fulfillment, and freedom that
I have been looking for in life.*

Today's Prayer
*Father, open my eyes to see Your immense love and heart of
compassion for me. Cut through any wrong beliefs that have kept me
in fear, guilt, and insecurity. Fill my heart every day with Your love.
I believe that in You I will find the joy, confidence, fulfillment,
and freedom my heart longs for. Amen.*

Today's Reflection on Right Believing

....

....

....

....

....

....

DAY 88

The Intimate Love of the Father

Today's Scripture

"I will be a Father to you, and you shall be My sons and daughters, says the LORD Almighty."
2 CORINTHIANS 6:18

Not too long ago, Lydia, a sister from South Africa, wrote to me. I believe that many of you would be able to identify with what she shared about her struggles in relating to God as her Father:

Dear Pastor Prince,

I grew up with very low self-esteem, having been labeled the difficult child in my family. I was an unplanned baby, and my parents already had one child—a girl, so they really wanted a boy. They were disappointed when I turned out to be a girl and even considered giving me to a paternal family member who did not have children.

My dad comes from a very cold, strict family, and he has a very bad temper, so I grew up naturally fearful of him and always felt like I was walking on eggshells around him. My mom also grew up in a household where she had not received love. Both my parents are extreme perfectionists, very organized, and raised us with military discipline and no compassion.

Thus, I could never relate to God as a Father. God was unapproachable and sitting with a lightning bolt ready to strike me whenever I wasn't good enough, didn't pray enough, or wasn't obedient enough. I was under the impression that God was only pleased with me when I obeyed the law, that I never met His expectations, and I was always under condemnation.

Since encountering your teaching resources, the veil in my life has been torn. For the first time, I am free. I no longer walk under the heavy burden of condemnation. I learned that God loved us first, and I can now have a love relationship with my heavenly Father and Jesus.

I have experienced victory over fear and sin that kept me captive for years—not by trying to be obedient, but by just learning that my sins have already been forgiven on the cross. And no, I am not sinning more now. I am actually overcoming more and sinning less, and I have a grateful heart for what Christ has done on the cross.

Do you feel as though you are never good enough, can never do enough and be obedient enough for God to love and accept you? Do you feel you are always living under perpetual condemnation? Perhaps you can't relate to God as a loving Father because you've never experienced the love of your earthly father or because your own father has hurt you terribly.

My friend, I pray that as we study the Word of God together, you will supernaturally experience the intimate love of your heavenly Father in a deep and personal way as never before. I pray that this experience will heal, renew, restore, and transform you in a spectacular way because His love for you is nothing less than spectacular.

Today's Thought

The more I open my heart to experience the intimate love of my heavenly Father in a deep and personal way, the more I will experience healing, renewal, restoration, and transformation in a spectacular way.

Today's Prayer

Father, thank You for making me and calling me Your child. Because of Your spectacular love for me, I never have to be good enough, do enough, or be obedient enough to be accepted by You. I believe and declare that Jesus, by His sacrifice, is my acceptance before You today. I open my heart to receive Your deep and intimate love for me, and I believe You are now healing, restoring, and transforming me effortlessly from the inside out. Amen.

Today's Reflection on Right Believing

DAY 89

See the Father's Perfect Love

Today's Scripture

"For God so loved the world that He gave His only begotten Son, that whoever believes in Him should not perish but have everlasting life."
JOHN 3:16

Under the new covenant of His amazing grace, your Father in heaven isn't looking to judge you for your failings because He has already judged your every failing, mistake, and sin in the body of His own Son, Jesus Christ. The name that Jesus came to reveal in the new covenant of grace is "Father." Today God wants to reach out to you as a caring and loving Father.

Do you know the extent of His heart of love toward you?

Did you know that it was His idea to send Jesus to be punished at the cross for you?

Read the most famous passage in the Bible and personalize it so that you can see God's heart for *you*: "For God so loved *you* that He gave His only begotten Son, that *you* who believe in Him should not perish but have everlasting life. For God did not send His Son into the world to condemn *you*, but that *you* through Him might be saved" (John 3:16–17). Know beyond the shadow of a doubt today that your Father loves *you* and sent His own Son to save *you*.

Understand that we are not belittling the work of Jesus at the cross when we talk about the Father and His love for you. The truth is Jesus came to reveal the love of the Father to you. God so loved you that He sent His one and only beloved Son to pay the heavy price at the cross to cleanse you of all your sins.

Do you know that God loves Jesus dearly? Jesus is God's darling Son, the apple of His eye. Now, if your Father in heaven didn't withhold His precious Son, Jesus Christ, and sacrificed Him for you, how much do you think He loves you? You cannot begin to comprehend the intensity and sheer magnitude of your Father's love for you until you realize how much the Father loves Jesus—because He gave up Jesus to ransom you.

I hope you are beginning to experience and see for yourself just how loved you are by the Father and how precious you are to Him! Don't fear Him—see the heart of your Father's love unveiled through Calvary's cross.

Today's Thought

My Father in heaven so loves me that He gave His only begotten, darling Son, Jesus, to die on the cross to save and ransom me.

Today's Prayer

Father, thank You that You are showing me the heart of Your love unveiled through Calvary's cross. I praise You for how much You love me and for showing me how precious I am to You. I believe that You gave Your darling Son to die on the cross for me so that I might experience Your saving grace and the depths of Your love every day. Amen.

Today's Reflection on Right Believing

DAY 90

Know Your Father's Heart

Today's Scripture

Herein is love, not that we loved God, but that he loved us,
and sent his Son to be the propitiation for our sins.
1 JOHN 4:10 KJV

Today, I want you to reread the parable of the father of the prodigal son (Luke 15:11–32). As you read, keep in mind that this son utterly rejected and completely humiliated and dishonored his father, then only returned home when he remembered that even his father's hired servants had more food than he did! It was not the son's love for his father that made him journey home; it was his stomach. In his own self-absorbed pride, he wanted to earn his own keep as a hired servant rather than to receive his father's provision by grace or unmerited favor.

God wants us to know that even when our motivations are wrong, even when we have a hidden (usually self-centered) agenda and our intentions are not completely pure, He still runs to us in our time of need and showers His unmerited, undeserved, and unearned favor upon us. Oh, how unsearchable are the depths of His love and grace toward us! It will never be about our love for God. It will always be about His magnificent love for us. The Bible makes this clear: "Herein is love, not that we loved God, but that he loved us, and sent his Son to be the propitiation for our sins" (1 John 4:10 KJV).

Some people think that fellowship with God can only be restored when you are perfectly contrite and have perfectly confessed all your sins. Yet we see in this parable that it was the father who was the initiator, it was the father who had missed his son, who was already looking out for him, and who had *already* forgiven him. Before the son could utter a single word of his rehearsed apology, the father had already run to him, embraced him, and welcomed him home. Can you see how it's all about our Father's heart of grace, forgiveness, and love? Our Father God swallows up all our imperfections, and true repentance comes because of His goodness.

Do I say "sorry" to God and confess my sins when I have fallen short and failed? Of course I do. But I do it not to be forgiven because I *know* that I am *already* forgiven through Jesus' finished work. The confession is out of the overflow of my heart because I have experienced His goodness and grace and because I know that as His son, I am forever righteous through Jesus' blood. It springs from being righteousness-conscious, not sin-conscious; from being forgiveness-conscious, not judgment-conscious. There is a massive difference.

If you understand this and begin practicing this, you will begin experiencing new dimensions in your love walk with the Father. You will realize that your Daddy God is all about relationship and not religious protocol. He just loves being with you. Under grace, He doesn't demand perfection from you; He *supplies* perfection to you through the finished work of His Son, Jesus Christ. So no matter how many mistakes you have made, don't be afraid of Him. He loves you. Your Father is running toward you to embrace you!

Today's Thought
My Father God runs to me in my time of need and showers His unmerited, undeserved, and unearned favor upon me.

Today's Prayer
Father, thank You that I can experience Your love even when I have failed. No matter how many mistakes I may have made, I don't have to be afraid to come to You. I am still Your beloved child, and I always have fellowship with You because of the finished work of Jesus. I thank You that You don't demand perfection from me, but You supply perfection to me through the cross. It blesses my heart to know that You just love being with me. Thank You for running to embrace me. Amen.

Today's Reflection on Right Believing

DAY 91

"Abba, Father!"

Today's Scripture

*For you did not receive the spirit of bondage again to fear,
but you received the Spirit of adoption by whom we cry out,
"Abba, Father." The Spirit Himself bears witness with our
spirit that we are children of God.*
ROMANS 8:15–16

I love it when I'm in Israel and I hear little children running around in playgrounds, calling out, "Abba! Abba!" and jumping into their daddies' embraces. To the Jews, *Abba* is the most intimate way in which you can address your father. It's a beautiful picture of the truth that through Jesus, you have received the Spirit of sonship by whom you cry out "Abba, Father." Did you notice that the Holy Spirit refused to translate the original Aramaic word "Abba" into English?

In Abba's arms, a child is most secure, protected, and loved. No enemy can pull a child out of his or her Abba's strong arms. That's the image God wants us to have when we pray to Him and call Him "Abba." Of course, you can call Him "Daddy" or "Papa," or whatever term helps you to see God as a warm, loving, and caring Father.

Unless you can see Him as your Abba Father, you will continue to have a "spirit of bondage again to fear" (Rom. 8:15), referring to the Old Testament fear of God. It's a slavish fear of judgment and punishment that brings you into bondage and makes you afraid of God. But God doesn't want you to fear Him. He wants you to have a Spirit of sonship! Too many believers are living with an orphan, fatherless spirit. If you are entangled with all kinds of fears, guilt, and worries today, what you need is a good heavenly dose of the Father's love for you!

Something amazing happens in your spirit when you see God as your Father. If my daughter, Jessica, has a nightmare, all she has to do is cry out, "Daddy!" and Daddy is there! Jessica doesn't have to go, "O Father that liveth and inhabiteth the next room, I plead with thee to come to me at this time of peril, that thou mayest rescue me from this nightmare!" All she has to do is to cry out, "Daddy!" and I'm there.

Similarly, in your moments of weakness you don't have to approach God with perfect prayers. You just cry out, "Daddy!" and your heavenly Father runs to you! You are not coming before a judge. You are coming before your Father, your Daddy God, who embraces and loves you just the way you are.

Take time to come to your Abba Father today. Believe that He loves you unconditionally today. See Him welcoming you with a smile on His face and with outstretched arms. Run into His embrace, bask in His perfect love for you, and let it melt away every worry, fear, and insecurity. When you believe and receive your Father's love for you, it will put unshakable peace and strength in your heart!

Today's Thought

What I need every day is a good heavenly dose of my Father's love for me!

Today's Prayer

Abba, Father, I thank You that I have received the Spirit of sonship in Jesus. Thank You that I do not have to live with an orphan, fatherless spirit because You have poured out Your love on me. I believe that I can come to You anytime, with anything on my heart and cry out, "Daddy!" and You will always be there for me. Amen.

Today's Reflection on Right Believing

DAY 92

Clothed with the Robe of Righteousness

Today's Scripture

I will greatly rejoice in the LORD, my soul shall be joyful in my God;
for He has clothed me with the garments of salvation, He has covered
me with the robe of righteousness, as a bridegroom decks himself
with ornaments, and as a bride adorns herself with her jewels.
ISAIAH 61:10

After I had preached a message on the Father's love in my church, a young man who had been involved in many gang fights and had been in and out of prison numerous times came forward to receive Jesus as his Lord and Savior. He looked straight at the youth pastor and asked him somberly, "Can God forgive me for all the mistakes I've made?" The youth pastor affirmed him, saying, "The moment you came forward to receive Jesus into your life, your Father in heaven forgave you of all your sins and made you His child. Right now, that's who you are—His beloved child."

My friend, no matter how many times you have failed, how many mistakes you have made, and how terrible you think your sins are, the cleansing power and blood of your Savior, Jesus Christ, is greater than them all. God made this promise to you in His Word: "Though your sins are like scarlet, I will make them as white as snow. Though they are red like crimson, I will make them as white as wool" (Isa. 1:18 NLT). That's the power of the cross in your life. The moment you believe in Christ, all your sins are washed away once and for all and you are made as white as snow. Have you seen how snow dazzles in the sunlight? That's how your Father in heaven sees you right now, clothed with the gleaming robe of righteousness.

But Pastor Prince, what have I done to deserve this robe of righteousness?

Consider the prodigal son. What did the son do to deserve the father's embrace or the best robe that the father commanded his hired servants to bring for him (Luke 15:22)? Absolutely nothing.

The "best robe" is a picture of the robe of righteousness that your heavenly Father clothed you with when you received Jesus. This robe of righteousness is a *free gift*. You cannot earn it, work for it, or merit it. That is why everything we hear about what the father did to welcome his son home is a picture of our heavenly Father's amazing and unconditional grace.

Our part is to just believe in His goodness and wholeheartedly receive the abundance of grace and the gift of righteousness from Him to reign victoriously over every area of defeat in our lives. Please join me now in today's prayer.

Today's Thought
My Father in heaven sees me right now clothed with the gleaming robe of righteousness.

Today's Prayer
Dear Daddy God, I know that I have done nothing to deserve Your love and blessings in my life. Thank You for giving me grace that is so unmerited. I humbly receive the abundance of Your grace and Your precious gift of righteousness. In Jesus' name, Amen.

Today's Reflection on Right Believing

DAY 93

Come and Join the Dance

Today's Scripture

He who did not spare His own Son, but delivered Him up for us all,
how shall He not with Him also freely give us all things?
ROMANS 8:32

Today, I want us to consider the older brother in the parable of the prodigal's father. He got massively angry when he heard that his shameless sinner of a brother returning home was the reason there was music and dancing in his father's house. Look at what he said to his father: "Lo, these many years I have been serving you; I never transgressed your commandment at any time; and yet you never gave me a young goat, that I might make merry with my friends. But as soon as this son of yours came, who has devoured your livelihood with harlots, you killed the fatted calf for him" (Luke 15:29–30).

This son's response revealed what he believed about his father—that he was a hard taskmaster, and that he needed to be served before his approval could be won. He believed that he needed to earn his father's blessings. Clearly he missed the whole point of what it means to be a son. His eyes were not on his father's goodness, but on his own performance. He had a slavish mind-set and was persistently trying to please his father with his service and by the care he took not to transgress his father's commandments. He never understood the father's heart. Simply put, he never understood grace.

Unfortunately, there are many believers today who are like the older brother. Rather than receive the Father's perfect love and acceptance by grace, they try to earn His blessings. Instead of enjoying a love relationship between a Father and His child, they still live under this veil of the law. They hear the music and the dancing, and they don't understand it. They hear about their Father's amazing grace, and they can't comprehend it. They read stories of lives transformed by grace, and they can't accept it. To them, God is all about keeping commandments, service, obedience, and rewards.

Do you know what the father, who had left the party to seek out his older son, said in response to this son's complaint? "Son, you are always with me, and all that I have is yours" (Luke 15:31).

My friend, it's not about *your* love for God; it's about the Father's love for you. He is always the initiator. It has always been about *His* love for you. Don't live life mad, angry, guilty, and frustrated. Come into the Father's house and find rest for your soul. It's not about your own efforts. Your Father wants you to know that ALL He has is already yours—not because of your perfect performance, but because you are His child through Jesus' finished work.

Romans 8:32 declares, "He who did not spare His own Son, but delivered Him up for us all, how shall He not with Him also freely give us all things?" Daddy God has already *with Jesus* given you all things. Jesus is your acceptance, righteousness, holiness, provision, and wisdom. Whatever it is you need in your life, your Father has already given to you through Jesus.

So come home to His embrace. Come home to grace. Come and join in the music and dancing!

Today's Thought
My heavenly Father wants me to enjoy a love relationship with Him, not one where I try to earn His blessings.

Today's Prayer
Father, thank You that all that You have is already mine because I am Your child through Jesus' finished work. Your Word tells me that You have already given me all things with Jesus, including whatever it is I need today. I believe that in Jesus I am accepted, righteous, and beloved, and I thank You that I can always depend on Your love. Amen.

Today's Reflection on Right Believing

DAY 94

Transformed by the Father's Love

Today's Scripture

If anyone loves the world, the love of the Father is not in him.
1 JOHN 2:15

*P*astor Prince, are you saying then that everything is just by grace and we can live any way we want with total disregard for God? Are you saying that we don't have to serve Him?

Well, ask yourself this: When someone genuinely encounters the Father's love, favor, and blessings in a way that is totally undeserving, how do you think he or she will live?

Take a moment to put yourself in the shoes of the prodigal son. After all the wrongs you have committed against your father, he gives you a lavish reception filled with hugs and kisses. You just went from starving to being clothed with a fresh, clean robe and wearing the ring of your father, authorizing you to make payments in his name. And as if that is not enough, your father has invited all the neighbors, killed a choice calf, and they are having a homecoming barbecue party with music and dancing in your honor.

Now, does this make you want to rebel against your father again by leaving home and going back to the filthy pigpen, wallowing in the mud and feeding on things that will never satisfy you? Of course not!

There is a great misunderstanding that believers who struggle with and indulge in sin, and who are still in love with the world, do so because they don't love God enough. Believers are told to love God more, thinking that if people love God more, they would love sin and the world less.

But God opened my eyes one day to the real reason believers are still entangled with sin and the world. I've never heard anyone preach this before, so this is fresh from heaven. The apostle John tells us, "If anyone loves the world, the love of the Father is not in him" (1 John 2:15). Notice that it is the love *of* the Father, not the love *for* the Father. So people who love the world and are trapped by worldly pursuits are actually people who don't know or don't believe in their hearts the love of the Father for them.

Rather than messages of "You've got to love God more!" what we really need is more preaching that is all about the love *of* the Father. It will never be about our love for Him, but *His* love for us.

Beloved, when people come to truly know and believe the Father's love for them and have it burning in their hearts, they will no longer want to go out and live like the devil. There is just something powerfully transformative about grace. That's what right believing in the Father's love brings. If you've tasted and savored grace from your heavenly Father, you never want to live in the wilderness of sin, away from the Father's embrace, ever again.

Today's Thought

It will never be about my love for God, but His love for me.

Today's Prayer

Father, thank You for the transformative power of Your grace and Your love in my life. You have taken me out of the wilderness of sin and brought me into Your tender embrace. I believe in Your love for me and want it to burn in my heart forever. I believe that as I embrace Your love for me, You will change me effortlessly. Amen.

Today's Reflection on Right Believing

....

....

....

....

....

....

....

....

....

DAY 95

Already Beloved, Already Qualified

Today's Scripture

See how very much our Father loves us, for he calls us
his children, and that is what we are!
1 JOHN 3:1 NLT

I received an awesome testimony from twenty-five-year-old Nathan from New York, who grew up with no father figure in his life except a man whom his mother married and who beat him regularly from the time he was three. Nathan struggled with his identity, his addictions, and his anger. But his turning point came when he learned that his Daddy God loves him. He wrote:

> *I heard a sermon of yours about being God's beloved. I had never heard someone speak about Jesus as someone who died for my sins because He loved me so much. I thought there was no way anyone would die for me if they knew what I'd done. But the love I felt as I listened was something I'd never experienced before.*
>
> *I had to know more, so I bought your book* Destined To Reign, *and the Lord's words through your book changed my life…. I've dropped every bad habit—everything—in my past and have given myself to the Lord Jesus Christ. Every day seems new to me, and I see life in a different light now. I know that I have a Father in heaven who loves and accepts me. I know that He hears my prayers and won't be slow to answer them.*

In the same way, I pray you will have a revelation that you are right now loved by the Father and close to His heart. That your Daddy God always hears your prayers and is more than able and willing to lift you out of every dark pit and set you in His love and light.

Right now, I want you to do something: close your eyes and just say, "Daddy."

That's a prayer right there. In fact, that's the deepest, most intimate prayer you can pray. Call upon your Daddy God because He loves you and cares for you. You never did anything to make Him fall in love with you. And beloved, there is nothing you can do, nothing you could have done, that will ever take away His love for you.

I want you to know today that as a child of God, you don't need to qualify for His love in any way. You are *already* His beloved. You may feel that you are far away from Him, but your Father sees you. He has been watching and waiting for you to come home, ready to sprint toward you to embrace you. He wants to lavish His love and kisses on you, over and over again.

You don't need to earn your Daddy's love. ALL that He has is already yours. He's not asking you to serve Him in order to earn His blessings. ALL that He has, He has already freely and unconditionally given to you.

He gave up His only Son to die an agonizing death on the cross for the chance that you might one day accept His love. So come. Come to the Father. Come with all your failings, with all your brokenness, with all your inadequacies.

Come as you are. As you realize that you are the object of His love, I pray that whatever is negative or destructive will be flushed out from your life and you will experience breakthrough after breakthrough like never before.

Today's Thought
Right now I am greatly loved by the Father and close to His heart.

Today's Prayer
Daddy God, thank You that I don't have to qualify for or earn Your love. You love me and care for me despite all my failings, brokenness, and inadequacies. I thank You that nothing will ever take away Your love for me, and I receive all that You have already freely and unconditionally given to me through Jesus' finished work. Amen.

Today's Reflection on Right Believing

DAY 96

Find Rest in the Father's Love

Today's Scripture

*"Though the mountains be shaken and the
hills be removed, yet my unfailing love for you will not
be shaken nor my covenant of peace be removed,"
says the LORD, who has compassion on you.*
ISAIAH 54:10 NIV

In these last days of our journey in discovering the power of right believing, I want to leave you with one simple but critical truth. Memorize this truth. Feed on it. Let it take root in your spirit and become an anchor in your life. You will never be the same again.

Are you ready? Here it goes:

> *As a child of God, no matter what happens in your life, your Father in heaven loves you dearly and nothing you do can ever change that.*

Will you believe that today? Whether you are going through good times or facing challenging times, you need to know that your Abba loves you. There is nothing that you can ever do to make Him love you more, and nothing that you can ever do to make Him love you less. Even—or perhaps *especially*—when you feel like you have failed, know that you will *always* be the apple of His eye. *Always.*

God loves you with an everlasting love (see Jer. 31:3). A love that is the same yesterday, today, forever. Feel your Daddy God enfolding you in His embrace right now. You are safe. You are utterly loved and completely accepted. He loved you before you ever knew Him. His love for you has *nothing* to do with anything that you have done for Him. *Nothing* you do will ever affect His unwavering, unconditional love for you.

There is nothing for you to prove. You only need to rest and receive your Abba's love. Let your life become established and grounded in a love that is so perfect that no challenge or adversity will be able to knock you down. If you think that you've messed up, turn to your Father. In His loving arms you will find hope, security, and refuge from any storm.

I love how the apostle Paul puts it: "Who shall separate us from the love of Christ? Shall tribulation, or distress, or persecution, or famine, or nakedness, or peril, or sword?… Yet in all these things we are more than conquerors through Him who loved us. For I am persuaded that neither death nor life, nor angels nor principalities nor powers, nor things present nor things to come, nor height nor depth, nor any other created thing, shall be able to separate us from the love of God which is in Christ Jesus our Lord" (Rom. 8:35, 37–39).

Beloved, there are no caveats or disclaimers when it comes to the love of your heavenly Father. The Bible plainly states that *nothing* shall be able to separate you from the love of your Father in heaven. It's an absolute declaration and promise. "Nothing" means *nothing*. As a believer, this means that even your mistakes, failings, and sins cannot separate you from the love of your Father. Hallelujah!

Today's Thought
I only need to rest and receive my Abba's love.

Today's Prayer
Father, You are my Abba, my Daddy God, who loved me
unconditionally before I ever knew You or anything about You.
I acknowledge today that I am utterly loved and completely accepted
by You. I believe that absolutely nothing can ever separate me
from Your love, and I rest in Your unchanging, unwavering,
and unshakable love for me. Amen.

Today's Reflection on Right Believing

....

....

....

....

....

....

DAY 97

Knowing Your Value Makes a Difference

Today's Scripture

Now may our Lord Jesus Christ Himself and God our Father, Who loved us and gave us everlasting consolation and encouragement and well-founded hope through [His] grace (unmerited favor), comfort and encourage your hearts and strengthen them [make them steadfast and keep them unswerving] in every good work and word.

2 Thessalonians 2:16–17 AMP

It is the Father's love for you that gives you the power to overcome every mistake, failure, and sin in your life. The Bible puts it this way: "Sin is no longer your master, for you no longer live under the requirements of the law. Instead, you live under the freedom of God's grace" (Rom. 6:14 NLT). Isn't that beautiful? Today you are living under the freedom of God's amazing grace—His unmerited, undeserved, and unearned favor in your life. Grace gives you freedom. Freedom from lack, from fear, from addictions, from the torment of guilt, and from every curse and every sin! The more you experience the love and grace of your heavenly Father, the more you fall in love with Him and out of love with sin.

Did you know that the enemy has no hold over people who know their Father loves them? If Adam and Eve had believed in God's love for them, the devil would not have been successful in tempting them. Unfortunately, they chose to believe the lie that the serpent had planted by portraying God as stingy and selfish, as if He was withholding something good from them.

That's why I want you to be anchored in the Father's love. You will be unshakable. You will have no desire to touch certain things, go to certain places, or be associated with certain people. You will keep away from negative influences because you trust your Father's heart for you and believe that He only wants what's best for you. You rest, knowing that He is watching out for you to protect you and insulate you from harm.

I've seen that children who are secure in their father's love are able to say no to all kinds of temptations. This is because that vacuum in their lives is already filled. They don't have to do things to win the approval of their friends when they can find absolute security, identity, and approval in their parents' love for them and, most of all, in their heavenly Father's love for them.

In the same way, when we trust in our Father's love for us, we will have the power to say no to temptations. When you have an abiding revelation of just how valuable, precious, and righteous you are in Christ, it becomes increasingly easy to say no to sin. The more righteousness-conscious you are and the more conscious of how valuable and precious you are in Christ, the more you will know that your righteous identity in Christ and sin don't go together—and the more you will experience the power to say no to temptation.

Today's Thought

When I'm anchored in the Father's love, I will be unshakable.

Today's Prayer

Father, thank You that I can live under the freedom of Your amazing grace. Thank You for the power to overcome every mistake, failure, and sin in my life. I believe that I am anchored in Your love and empowered to say no to temptation because I receive and rest in Your love. In Jesus' name, Amen.

Today's Reflection on Right Believing

DAY 98

You Are Beloved and Well Pleasing

Today's Scripture

When He had been baptized, Jesus came up immediately from the water; and behold, the heavens were opened to Him, and He saw the Spirit of God descending like a dove and alighting upon Him. And suddenly a voice came from heaven, saying, "This is My beloved Son, in whom I am well pleased."
MATTHEW 3:16–17

After Jesus' baptism, the Holy Spirit led Him into the wilderness, and the devil came to tempt Him saying, "If You are the Son of God, command that these stones become bread" (Matt. 4:3).

Many years ago when I was studying this, the Lord opened my eyes and showed me that the devil had subtly left out the word "beloved." Just moments ago, God the Father had just affirmed Jesus as His *beloved* Son at the Jordan River. However, when the devil came to tempt Jesus, he removed the word "beloved" and simply said, "If You are the Son of God…"

The Lord unveiled to me that if you are reminded that you are the beloved of the Father, you can never be successfully tempted! Even the devil knew this, and that's why he removed the word "beloved" when he spoke to Jesus. Now that's a powerful truth!

So every time you are tempted, just remind yourself, "I am God's beloved child, and my Father loves me." No temptation can triumph over you when you rest securely in your Father's love.

Now observe Jesus' reply. He didn't have to prove to the devil that He was the Son of God. Secure in His identity as God's beloved Son, He simply replied, "It is written, 'Man shall not live by bread alone, but by every word that proceeds from the mouth of God'" (Matt. 4:4). And what words had the Father just said at the Jordan River? *"This is My beloved Son, in whom I am well pleased."*

I want to encourage you to personalize this and meditate on it every day! That's how the Father sees you today. He sees you in Christ, and in Christ you are His precious, beloved child, in whom He is well pleased. Place your hand on your heart and hear your Father in heaven saying these words to you:

"You are My beloved child, in whom I am well pleased."

Would you believe that with all your heart today? If you are struggling to overcome a disorder or addiction, close your eyes and hear your Father saying to you, "You are My beloved child, in whom I am well pleased." Every time you are fearful, every time you are consumed by worry, anger, or depression, hear your Father saying to you, "You are My beloved child, in whom I am well pleased."

Yes, right in the midst of whatever failures you may be experiencing, you are His beloved child, and He is well pleased with you because you are in Christ. Keep hearing it and repeating it until you find rest, peace, and joy overflowing in your heart. If you feel like just crying in His presence, cry. He knows what you are going through and He understands—in a way that no one else can—the pain, hurt, suffering, and loss that you are experiencing. Let His perfect love cast out every fear and bring healing and wholeness to your heart.

Today's Thought
My Father sees me in Christ, and in Christ I am His precious, beloved child, in whom He is well pleased.

Today's Prayer
Father, thank You that You see me in Jesus, and in Jesus I am Your precious, beloved child, in whom You are well pleased. Despite my failings and no matter what I may be experiencing today, I declare that I am Your beloved child, and You are well pleased with me because I am in Christ. I place my hand over my heart, and with my whole heart I choose to believe this powerful truth. Thank You, Father, for Your perfect love that casts out every fear, worry and anxiety in my heart. Amen.

Today's Reflection on Right Believing

....

....

DAY 99

You Are Accepted in the Beloved

Today's Scripture

...to the praise of the glory of His grace, by which He made us accepted in the Beloved. In Him we have redemption through His blood, the forgiveness of sins, according to the riches of His grace.

EPHESIANS 1:6–7

We saw yesterday that we are God's beloved and well pleasing to Him because we are in Christ.

But Pastor Prince, I have done nothing to make myself well pleasing to God!

Neither did Jesus. God called Jesus His beloved and said that He was well pleasing *before* He had even performed one miracle or act of service for Him. You see, Jesus is well pleasing to His Father not because of what He has *done*, but because of who He *is*. Did you get that? If not, please read the last sentence again.

Jesus didn't have to do anything or accomplish anything before He was considered beloved and pleasing to the Father. The good news for you and me today is that our Father in heaven has "made us accepted in the Beloved," and "in Him we have redemption through His blood, the forgiveness of sins, according to the riches of His grace" (Eph. 1:6–7).

This is true for any believer of Jesus. The moment you received Him into your life, God the Father made you accepted in the Beloved.

We know that the word "Beloved" here is in reference to Jesus. So why didn't God just say "accepted in Jesus Christ"?

That is because God wants you to be conscious that you are now part of the family and you are *beloved* to Him the same way that Jesus is. Furthermore, the word "accepted" in the original Greek is a word far richer in meaning than the English translation can convey. It's the word *charitoo*, and it means "highly favored."[9] This word is used only one other time in the Bible, when angel Gabriel appeared to Mary and said to her, "Rejoice, highly favored [*charitoo*] one, the Lord is with you; blessed are you among women!" (Luke 1:28).

So you and I are not just accepted in the Beloved, which is already fantastic, but we are more precisely *highly favored* in the Beloved, Jesus Christ. In fact, the Greek scholar Thayer says that *charitoo* also means we are surrounded by favor.[10] That's why in my church we like to proclaim and declare that we are *highly favored*, *greatly blessed*, and *deeply loved*. It's a powerful declaration and an important reminder that you are not alone and left to fend for yourself in life. You have a Father in heaven who loves you, favors you, protects you, and watches over you and all your loved ones.

Today's Thought
I have a Father in heaven who loves me, favors me, protects me, and watches over me and all my loved ones.

Today's Prayer
Father, thank You that I am not just accepted in Jesus the Beloved, but I am also highly favored in Him. Thank You that I can abide under Your love, favor, and protection. I believe that I am highly favored, greatly blessed, and deeply loved by You today and always. Amen.

Today's Reflection on Right Believing

DAY 100

All This Freedom Can Be Yours

Today's Scripture

*And we have known and believed the love that God
has for us. God is love, and he who abides in love
abides in God, and God in him.*

1 JOHN 4:16

I love this heartfelt praise report I received from Gina, who lives in Maryland. Listen to how she has been transformed by the love of the Father:

Dear Pastor Prince,

I have been a Christian for about thirty-four years. Since discovering your teachings, I feel like I have been released from thirty-four years of being in a prison of Christian legalism, rules, and lists of things I had to do to get God to help and bless me.

Before hearing the unadulterated gospel of grace, I had all but given up on my life as a Christian. Yes, I still believed that I would go to heaven, but just barely. I didn't even pray anymore because I felt I had so many problems that I would probably not be praying right anyway, so why bother? I hated reading the Bible because to me it was just a reminder of all the things I was doing wrong and all the stuff I had to do if I wanted God's help.

But now I can't get enough of God's Word because I see it as a love letter from God rather than a book of rules that I can't keep. I also can't get enough of listening to the sermons that I get from you and feel like I have been given healthy, nourishing food after spending thirty-four years eating junk food. I listen to your sermons over and over again. I find myself spending more time in the Word because it is FINALLY really and truly GOOD NEWS that I am hearing. I want to know more about who God is for real.

For the first time in my life, my kids, who are in their twenties, are EXCITED about God too. We are all reading Destined To Reign *and constantly listening to teachings from your ministry. Recently I was thinking about the God whom I now know as my Abba Father, and I felt overwhelmed by His love for me. I started to say, "I love You." Suddenly I realized there are just no words to adequately convey the love I feel for Him now. Those three little words just don't cover it. Sometimes I feel like my heart will burst from the love I feel for Him now because I finally believe He feels the same way about me!*

Additionally, things that I have been trying to quit for DECADES are now beginning to just fade away as I rest in God knowing He's going to keep loving me no matter what. Who knew that NOT trying to "be good" would bring about a heart change and then change me on the outside too. I cannot believe all this has been available to me all along.

I am so happy now that I can't even describe it. Yes, I am still having my share of challenges, but things look so much different when you know that God not only CAN handle it, but He WILL handle it when you just rest and let Him be the Daddy to you that He wants to be.

I cannot thank you enough for your ministry and your obedience to God in bringing this life-changing Word to us, His children. I have been forever changed, and I tell everybody about the gospel of grace that you preach. God is so wonderful, and I look forward to the next seventy years of my life walking in His grace and sharing it with His people.

When you see and believe the Father's love and grace shining on you, darkness fades away. Depression, eating disorders, suicidal thoughts, fears, and destructive addictions fade away. The more you place yourself under His grace, the more sin will have no dominion over you. Temptation will have no power over you when you are saturated with the Father's love, approval, favor, and acceptance. All this freedom can be yours when you truly believe this: *You are His beloved child, in whom He is well pleased.*

Here is my prayer for you, my friend. I pray that you will begin to comprehend and believe the width and length and depth and height of your Father's unconditional love for you. Rest in your Father's love for you and not your love for Him. And may you experience victory over every fear, every sense of guilt, and every addiction in your life.

Today's Thought

Not only can God handle my challenges, but He WILL handle them when I simply rest and let Him be the Daddy that He wants to be to me.

Today's Prayer

Father, thank You for the power of right believing and all that You are doing in my life through these 100 days of receiving Your grace and love. I believe that You are opening my eyes to see and believe the width and length and depth and height of Your unconditional love for me. I look forward to a lifetime of victories in Jesus' name. Amen.

Today's Reflection on Right Believing

Endnotes

[1] Cornwall, Judson and Michael Reid. *Whose Love Is It Anyway?* Closter, New Jersey: Sharon Publications, 1991. pp. 58–59.

[2] NT: 1343, *Vine's Expository Dictionary of Biblical Words.* Copyright © 1985, Thomas Nelson Publishers.

[3] NT: 4991, *Thayer's Greek Lexicon,* Electronic Database. Copyright © 2000, 2003, 2006 by Biblesoft, Inc. All rights reserved.

[4] NT: 1680, *Vine's Expository Dictionary of Biblical Words.* Copyright © 1985, Thomas Nelson Publishers.

[5] OT: 2617, *Vine's Expository Dictionary of Biblical Words.* Copyright © 1985, Thomas Nelson Publishers.

[6] OT: 3258, *The Online Bible Thayer's Greek Lexicon and Brown, Driver, & Briggs Hebrew Lexicon.* Copyright © 1993, Woodside Bible Fellowship, Ontario, Canada. Licensed from the Institute for Creation Research.

[7] Retrieved May 3, 2013, from www.nlm.nih.gov/medlineplus/ency/article/003647.htm.

[8] OT: 2617, *Vine's Expository Dictionary of Biblical Words.* Copyright © 1985, Thomas Nelson Publishers.

[9] NT: 5487, *Biblesoft's New Exhaustive Strong's Numbers and Concordance with Expanded Greek-Hebrew Dictionary.* Copyright © 1994, 2003, 2006 by Biblesoft, Inc. and International Bible Translators, Inc.

[10] NT: 5487, *Thayer's Greek Lexicon,* Electronic Database. Copyright © 2000, 2003, 2006 by Biblesoft, Inc. All rights reserved.

SPECIAL APPRECIATION

*Special thanks and appreciation to all who have
sent in their testimonies and praise reports to us.
Kindly note that all testimonies are received in good
faith and edited only for brevity and fluency.
Names have been changed to protect
the writers' privacy.*

STAY CONNECTED WITH JOSEPH

Connect with Joseph through these social media channels, and receive daily inspirational teachings:

Facebook.com/Josephprince
Twitter.com/Josephprince
Youtube.com/Josephprinceonline

Prayer Request

If you have a prayer request, you can share it with our online community at **Gracehope.com/Josephprince**. Our prayer teams are on standby to pray with you.

Free Daily Email Devotional

Sign up for Joseph's FREE daily email devotional at **JosephPrince.com/meditate** and receive bite-sized inspirations to help you grow in grace.

Salvation Prayer

If you would like to receive all that Jesus has done for you and make Him your Lord and Savior, please pray this prayer:

Lord Jesus, thank You for loving me and dying for me on the cross. Your precious blood washes me clean of every sin. You are my Lord and my Savior, now and forever. I believe You rose from the dead and that You are alive today. Because of Your finished work, I am now a beloved child of God and heaven is my home. Thank You for giving me eternal life and filling my heart with Your peace and joy. Amen.

We Would Like to Hear from You

If you have prayed the salvation prayer or if you have a testimony to share after reading this book, please send us an email at praise@josephprince.com.

BOOKS BY JOSEPH PRINCE

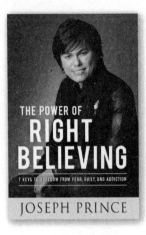

A *New York Times* Best Seller

THE POWER OF RIGHT BELIEVING

Experience transformation, breakthroughs, and freedom today through the power of right believing! Debuting at #2 on *The New York Times* Best Seller list, *The Power of Right Believing* offers seven practical and powerful keys that will help you find freedom from all fears, guilt, and addictions. See these keys come alive in the many precious testimonies you will read from people around the world who have experienced breakthroughs and liberty from all kinds of bondages. Win the battle for your mind through understanding the powerful truths of God's Word and begin a journey of victorious living and unshakable confidence in God's love for you!

DESTINED TO REIGN

This pivotal and quintessential book on the grace of God will change your life forever! Join Joseph Prince as he unlocks critical foundational truths to understanding God's grace and how it alone sets you free to experience victory over every adversity, lack, and destructive habit that is limiting you today. Be uplifted and refreshed as you discover how reigning in life is all about Jesus and what He has already done for you. Get your copy today and start experiencing the success, wholeness, and victory that you were destined to enjoy!

JOSEPH**PRINCE**.COM